DO THE IMPOSSIBLE

DO THE IMPOSSIBLE

Unlock Your Full Potential
with the Power of Mindset

Jason Drees

BiggerPockets®
PUBLISHING
Denver, Colorado

Do The Impossible : Unlock Your Full Potential With The Power Of Mindset
Jason Drees

Published by BiggerPockets Publishing LLC, Denver, CO
Copyright © 2021 by Jason Drees
All Rights Reserved.

Publisher's Cataloging-in-Publication Data

Names: Drees, Jason, author.
Title: Do the impossible : unlock your full potential with the power of mindset / Jason Drees.
Description: Denver, CO: BiggerPockets Publishing, 2022.
Identifiers: LCCN: 2021949917 | ISBN: 9781947200647 (hardcover) | 9781947200654 (ebook)
Subjects: LCSH Success--Psychological aspects. | Success in business. | Self-actualization (Psychology) | Self-help. | BISAC BUSINESS & ECONOMICS / Personal Success | SELF-HELP / Motivational & Inspirational | SELF-HELP / Personal Growth / Success | BUSINESS & ECONOMICS / Motivational
Classification: LCC BF637.S8 D74 2022 | DDC 158/.1--dc23

Printed on recycled paper in the United States of America
10 9 8 7 6 5 4 3 2 1

Dedication

To my beautiful wife *Alexis*, whose love and support made the journey to uncover the content in this book possible. I could not have done it without you.

To *Dash*, for your curiosity, playfulness, and willingness to follow me and try new things. Being your dad brings me more love and joy than I can describe.

To *Magnus*, for your strength, maturity, and authenticity. You always show me that the best person you can ever be is yourself. I'm proud to be your dad.

To *Leo*, who has the biggest heart of any person I know. The way you care and stand up for others is exactly what is needed in the world today. You fill my heart with joy and wonder.

To *Ace*, the bold leader with a powerful presence. I love spending time with you and am excited to see the amazing things you're going to do in life.

TABLE OF CONTENTS

FOREWORD

"I didn't know that wasn't the way it was supposed to be done."

That was the answer I received from my good friend Kevin when I begged him to tell me how he fix-and-flipped more than *one-hundred* homes in his first year as a real estate investor.

"Wait," I said, not sure I'd heard him correctly. "You didn't know that flipping one-hundred houses in your first year wasn't the norm?"

"Nope," he replied. "It just kind of happened."

At this point in the conversation, I'm pretty sure my mouth hit the floor. After all, I had just spent the previous six months trying to fix-and-flip *one* single-family home and struggling every day at it—and this was my fifth or sixth year in the business. I'd come home covered in sawdust, blood, and sweat; cram in the recording of a podcast episode; and try to spend some time binge-watching a Netflix show with my wife, only to sleep far-too-few hours and do it all again the next day.

Now, Kevin is a smart guy. But he wasn't rolling in cash, nor was he flush with some secret source of deals. He didn't have a Harvard MBA, come from a management background, or live in the world's best location to fix-and-flip houses. In fact, from what I could see, Kevin didn't have anything that would make him one-hundred times more successful than me.

And that's when it hit me: Maybe the thing that separated us and made him so wildly successful wasn't something I could *see*. Maybe it was something different about the way he *thought*, something about the way he saw the world and faced problems.

That was the day I was confronted with the reality that seems so blatantly obvious to me now: Our results are not dictated simply by superior knowledge, immense previous experience, or even massive actions. The results we obtain—or fail to obtain—are directed primarily by that tiny piece of real estate between our ears. In other words, our *results are shaped by our mindset.*

Mindset is the way we view the world; more specifically, mindset is the way we view problems. My friend Kevin had a very different mindset than I did when building a real estate business, as showcased in the way he handled the "problem" of a fix-and-flip. My mindset said, "Pick up a hammer." His mindset said, "Pick up the phone and build a team." These mindsets led to very different strategies, which led to very different actions, which led in turn to very different results.

Once I noticed that it was an internal issue that was holding me back from doing more, I naturally asked Kevin a very simple but life-changing question: "I want to shift my mindset to think more like you do. Do you know any coaches who specialize in this?"

And his answer forever changed my life: *Jason Drees.*

Kevin, I came to find out, had been working with a performance coach, Jason Drees, for some time. Each week, they would sit down and talk about the problems in Kevin's life, and Jason would ask the right questions, probe, and offer subtle suggestions to get Kevin's mindset clear and focused.

After a brief introductory call, I agreed to meet with Jason every other week to do the same as Kevin. At first, I expected Jason to simply listen to my problems and then give me the solution. But that's not what happened. Instead, Jason dug in deeper to my problems—to my mindset—to get me into alignment.

Alignment is a term Jason will spend time in this book discussing; it has incredible power to make your pursuits easier and more fun. When you are aligned, life just flows.

The best example of alignment I can conjure is from the incredible film *Ferris Bueller's Day Off*, where everything (from getting his girlfriend out of school to singing in a downtown Chicago parade to sneaking back home before his parents discovered his rouse) simply *flowed* for Ferris. It worked out so effortlessly because Ferris was aligned in what he was doing. Imagine going through your life this way! Imagine if your marriage and other relationships *flowed*. Imagine if your business and investments *flowed*. Imagine if your spiritual life *flowed*. Imagine a world where your pursuits are not necessarily easy (after all, where's the fun in that?), but they are filled with excitement, passion, energy, and success! That's what alignment is; it's what Jason has taught me to operate within, and it's what you'll learn to get into throughout this book. When you learn to live in alignment, you can truly do incredible things—maybe even do the impossible.

When I look back on the past five-plus years of working with Jason, the impossible is exactly what I feel I've done. Not all at once, of course. But as I worked with Jason on my mindset, and as we began to shift my frames (a concept you'll encounter again and again throughout this book), it began to work. My life began to shift. Soon, the results started to compound in a truly remarkable way. To give a quick summary of some of those impossible-for-me feats, allow me the indulgence to brag for a moment:

- When I began working with Jason, I made just over $60,000 per year. Making $100,000 felt absurd. $200,000 felt impossible. Today, I make several million dollars per year.
- When I first started working with Jason, I had just crossed the line of owning $3 million in real estate. Owning $5 million felt crazy. Owning $30 million felt utterly impossible. Today, I have over $300 million in assets under management in my company, Open Door Capital.
- When I began working with Jason, I had sworn off ever raising money for real estate deals. I remember crying to him, "I can't raise money! I hate it. It sucks. No one wants to lend me money." In other words: It was impossible. As of today, I've raised over $100 million from investors who trust and believe in me. In fact, when a big real estate deal comes along, we typically raise tens of millions within several days—with a waitlist of hundreds of investors who didn't get in soon enough.
- When I first started working with Jason, I lived in one of the most depressed, gloomy counties in America (Grays Harbor, Washington). We had so many roots and family connections there; leaving was impossible. Today, I live in a gorgeous house overlooking the ocean in Maui, Hawaii, and I get to spend countless hours creating incredible memories for my family. Speaking of family...
- When I first started working with Jason, I had no children and desperately wanted some. In fact, the doctors told me having children would likely be impossible. Today, I have two beautiful kids and spend most of my days sharing this incredible world with them.

Here is the crazy thing: Most of this was not actually that difficult.

Yes, it required work. Often hard work. But because I worked with Jason on changing the mindset in which I attacked problems, rather than simply attacking the problems themselves, the results *flowed*. I found alignment, and the results followed. Today, money comes easier. Deals come easier. Wealth comes easier. Talented team members come easier. Giving comes easier. Teaching comes easier. Writing comes easier. Speaking comes easier. Being a good husband and father comes easier.

I'm not saying my life is perfect—far from it. I'm continually learning, evolving, and creating new versions of myself. Oftentimes, I slip out of the frame I want to be in and find myself temporarily in a disempowered state once again. (Thankfully, I have the tools needed to quickly dig out, as will you after finishing this book.) Overall, however, I find myself significantly more in alignment than I've ever been before. I can feel it. Others can feel it. And it feels good.

That's what this book is about to do for you. I believe everyone can create an incredible life for themselves, however they define it. But Jason takes it a step further and shows you how to make the creation of an incredible life a fun, fast, and sometimes even easy process. He'll show you exactly how to effortlessly change your mindset by easily and immediately shifting your frame. You'll learn how to develop clarity and confidence in setting big goals and knowing you'll be able to reach them. You'll gain the wisdom needed to begin creating your ideal life, and he'll give you the tools necessary to get there—plus so much more. And, unlike me, you won't need to spend half a decade and tens of thousands of dollars to learn it from Jason. It's here.

Sound exciting? It is! So, keep reading. The concepts in this book are not difficult to understand, but at the same time, they are likely very different from what you've heard or read in the past. You may encounter parts that make you feel a little "out there," like when you'll be asked to repeat certain phrases out loud. Do this. Trust me; it helps. You may also find terms or phrases that you don't fully understand. Don't run away; run toward. Seek to understand, and you will—even if it takes some time.

Let me shut up now and get you onto the good part—Jason's wisdom. I'll just close with this:

I believe in you. I believe in Jason. And I believe that together you can *do the impossible.*

To your success,

Brandon Turner
December 2021
Maui, HI

THIS ENTIRE BOOK IN ONE PAGE.

1. You are limitless. There is no limit to what you can do. You can be, learn, or do anything.

2. Speaking your reality out loud is the fastest way to change it.

3. The impossible is not impossible; it is just an uncommon target.

4. All the fear about the journey of becoming great disappears the moment you remove the option of not becoming great.

5. How to create your reality:

    FRAME ➡ MINDSET ➡ THOUGHTS ➡ STRATEGY
    ACTION ➡ RESULT

6. Limiting beliefs are indicators of misalignment, nothing more.

7. Picking the right target is just as important as hitting the target. Most people pick targets that are too low. If you are not excited about your target, it's the wrong target and probably not big enough. If you know exactly what to do, you aren't aiming high enough. The purpose of the impossible target is to *transform* you.

8. Life is always responding to you, based upon your frame. Life always brings you what you are matched to.

9. You can live your life in reaction, or you can live your life in creation. It's your choice.

10. The success formula:
    - *Move into an aligned frame.*
    - *Follow the process of life.*
    - *Get the result.*

11. The universe is mathematical. Effort and worthiness have nothing to do with it.

12. The human journey is an emotional one.

13. Emotions are your internal guidance system. You are supposed to follow them, not avoid them.

14. Certainty means you are aligned with your target. Uncertainty means you are not.

15. The present is the result of the past, not an indicator of the future. Anything can happen next.

16. Past models of success are limitations, not accelerators.

17. Success is the starting point, not the destination.

18. Obstacles are gateways to transformation.

19. There are only three reasons you don't have what you want:
    - *You have resistance or misalignment to the process of getting it.*
    - *You have resistance or misalignment to having it.*
    - *Life needs more time to bring it to you.*

PART ONE

REDEFINING THE IMPOSSIBLE

Chapter One

THE JOURNEY TO GREATNESS

Doing the impossible is the path to greatness.

Untapped greatness lies within you. Born with unbounded potential, you have the capacity to do the impossible, and it is inherent in every human being. Unfortunately, most of us have been conditioned to deny our birthright and settle for the status quo. Unwittingly, we believe greatness is reserved for a lucky few, and the exceptional are truly an exception, set apart by some fantastical, foreign ability. Everything that propels your heroes and role models to defy convention and dare to be great also exists in you. Are you ready to tap into your unbounded potential? Recognizing and igniting your inner flame of greatness is as simple as making a decision to explore your full potential.

Have you ever watched someone break a record during the Olympic Games? How did it make you feel? Watching others expand human potential through awesome acts and achievements stirs something inside of us, doesn't it? Connected to them by the joy of unbridled possibility, we feel pride and admiration because they embody the power of passionately pursuing life. We celebrate and honor "great people" (the seemingly select few) because they make their dreams their reality. Swelling with inspiration, endeared to them by our own inner (often untapped) greatness, we say things like, "Anything is possible when you put your mind to it."

Ignoring our own capacity for greatness, we return to accepting average results. Ironically, that tired cliché we tout when someone else does something amazing is the key to doing the impossible. Anything *is* possible when you align your mindset with greatness.

When you ask kids what they want to be when they grow up, most answer from a place of endless possibility. Astronaut, ballerina, pro athlete, fighter pilot, trapeze artist. Open to all the world has to offer, not yet limited by social conditioning, their youth sets them free. Do you remember that freedom?

As we move toward adulthood, we begin to see following our dreams as illogical and irresponsible. Cutting ourselves off from the world of our true desires, we deny our capacity for greatness. But it is never too late, no matter your age. In every moment, you have the choice to embrace that childlike, wide-open freedom and set your mind on becoming the exception.

The journey to greatness is not an easy road or a straight line, but neither is a life of settling for average. Over the past twenty years, I failed more than I succeeded. At times, it was extremely challenging. News flash: Whether you decide to be great or settle for being average, life is challenging. Average doesn't make life easier; it just makes it less exciting and not nearly as rewarding.

One simple reason more people don't aim for greatness is because they tried to follow a dream and initially failed. After encountering a stumbling block or two, they turned back to their comfort zone. To protect themselves, they chose to believe going smaller was the smarter, better choice. Inadvertently, many of us avoid greatness because we are scared to fail, when failing is an important part of the process. To embark on a journey to greatness we must embrace our failures and view them as significant stepping-stones to our destiny.

Taking a more objective view of failure helps to clear away unnecessary regret. By cleaning up our understanding of mismarked missteps, we are better prepared—and motivated—to face our future. We are better aligned with our journey to greatness. When we take the time to honor, understand, and integrate how we arrived at this moment, our past can become empowering as opposed to debilitating.

One thing I did not anticipate is how lonely the journey to greatness can be. When you start following your dreams and passions, you may not be supported initially, especially if your path contradicts what those around you believe. At least that has been my experience.

During my journey to becoming a coach and starting my own company, I was committed to doing something great. This scared people around me because it was unconventional. Only after I took action beyond my comfort zone countless times did I hit the target. When I looked around for acknowledgment, it seemed as if no one even witnessed my accomplishment. Undeterred, I began picking bigger targets and having greater success. Again, I looked around for acknowledgment and still found nothing. Instead, I was questioned, ridiculed, and directly asked why I was trying to sabotage my family.

People I love said, "What are you doing? Why would you leave a good-paying job? Why risk that security on a start-up? Why do you need to become a coach?" As much as that feedback hurt, I knew I was aligned with my destiny. I knew I had to continue; there was no other way. I knew that if I didn't follow through, I would be settling. And if I started settling, I might never stop.

When I finally began to receive acknowledgment for my achievements, it was no longer important to me. I realized the satisfaction of pursuing my passion unapologetically was vastly more rewarding than the approval of others. When I no longer needed external acknowledgment, I began to receive recognition. Life is funny that way.

My success is the result of an important decision. I decided that operating at less than my full potential was unacceptable. I can't pretend to understand your journey or life experience. But I know you've had challenges and obstacles. That said, I want you to accept this truth now: *You are capable of far more than you think you are.* You are capable of achieving more in life than you currently believe. Don't be afraid. All of the emotion and resistance you feel about pushing beyond your comfort zone begins to disappear the second you decide there is no other option.

Let's get into alignment. Answer these questions:

- Are you ready to walk the path to greatness?
- Are you open to the growth the path of greatness will create?
- Are you ready to live in the world of endless possibility?

Excellent, now let's integrate.

The integration process is simple. Repeat the following words out loud to bring the intention into reality.

Repeat After Me (out loud):

- *I take full ownership of my life and everything in it.*
- *I take full ownership of my past, present, and future.*
- *I acknowledge my capacity for greatness.*
- *I acknowledge and own the greatness within me.*
- *I choose to walk my path of greatness.*
- *I choose to remove the option of not becoming great.*
- *I take full ownership of anything blocking me from becoming great and release it all now.*
- *I choose to believe this 100 percent, past, present, and future—all versions of me. And I immediately take ownership of anything contradictory to this and release all of it now.*

Now we are at it, let's get into alignment with receiving the full impact of this book.

Repeat After Me (out loud):

- *I take full ownership of my life and everything in it.*
- *I take full ownership of my past, present, and future.*

- *I choose to explore the concepts and ideas in this book.*
- *I allow myself to easily adopt the ideas because I want to believe.*
- *I allow myself to easily let go of any patterns of belief or behavior that are in resistance to what I want to believe.*
- *I want to have more ease and flow in my life.*
- *I want to create more success with ease.*
- *I allow myself to create more success with ease.*
- *I take full ownership of anything blocking the ease and flow in my life and release it all now.*
- *I have more ease and flow in my life.*
- *I choose to live in a reality where I am able to create success with ease, even if I don't know how to in this moment.*
- *I choose to believe this 100 percent, past, present, and future—all versions of me. And I immediately take ownership of anything contradictory to this and integrate all of it now.*

Let's now move into alignment with immediate transformation, so we can grow and integrate faster than ever before.

Repeat After Me (out loud):

- *I take full ownership of my life and everything in it.*
- *I take full ownership of my past, present, and future.*
- *I understand that growth and transformation is possible for me and other people.*
- *I understand that the speed of growth and transformation can be fast or slow.*
- *I choose to explore the reality of immediate growth, transformation, and integration—because I want to.*
- *I can grow and transform whenever I want to.*
- *I choose to explore the mindset of immediate transformation that does not require additional work, focus, or effort to integrate or remember.*
- *I choose to understand that this is possible to do quickly because anything is possible in the next moment.*

- *I choose to explore the reality where I can grow as fast as I want to, without pain or struggle.*
- *I choose to explore the reality where growth can be easy, fun, and exciting.*
- *I choose to explore the reality where radical, accelerated 10X growth is the norm and is accessible to me anytime I want it to be.*
- *I believe this because I choose to, because I choose to explore my full potential.*
- *I choose to believe this 100 percent, past, present, and future—all versions of me. And I immediately take ownership of anything contradictory to this and integrate all of it now.*

Frame-Shifting Exercise

Imagine that you decide to walk your unique path to greatness.
- Can you get a sense of your future self that is walking your path to greatness?
- Can you get a sense of a version of you from the future who has been walking your unique path to greatness for one year?
- Can you get a sense of a version of you from the future who has been walking your unique path to greatness for ten years?

Pretend for a moment that you have moved into immediate transformation.
- Can you get a sense of a version of you from the future that grows and transforms with ease?

Imagine that you have mastered and integrated all the content in this book.
- Can you get a sense of your future self that understands everything in this book?
- Can you get a sense of a future version of you that has been living the principles in this book for five years?
- Can you get a sense of your future self that knows this book so well you can teach it to others?

Imagine you have mastered living a life of ease and flow.
- Can you get a sense of a future version of you that has been living in ease and flow for three months?
- Can you get a sense of your future self that has been living in ease and flow for ten years?

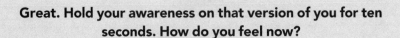

Great. Hold your awareness on that version of you for ten seconds. How do you feel now?

Do you feel lighter? Do you feel more prepared for walking your path and unlocking your full potential? Are you less afraid and more empowered? If you answer yes to even one of these questions, you just shifted frames.

Frame shifting is one of the primary tools I use to explain and expand mindset. We'll dive deeper into frame shifting later in the book, but for now just focus on approaching and engaging each exercise with an open mind. Monitor your experience without judging it or the process. After each exercise, simply ask yourself: Do I feel more aligned with what I want in life and better equipped to make it happen?

Chapter Two

DOING THE IMPOSSIBLE IS NOT IMPOSSIBLE

Only in retrospect do the defining moments of life become clear. In the present moment, point of view is limited. Our ability to see the big picture is often blocked by a swirl of emotion and past experience, especially when encountering something new or scary. Fear can overwhelm and cloud perspective. Feelings and thoughts of uncertainty distort the amazing nature of life's offerings. Recognizing the abundance, opportunity, and possibility in every moment can feel impossible when we are trapped under the pressure of the present. Though all of this is true, it does not have to be our reality.

Harnessing the power of mindset allows us to explore and optimize life's endless possibilities. It allows us to create our own reality. By shifting our mindset, we can stop seeing emotions as unwanted annoyances and embrace our feelings as invaluable guides.

Mindset shifting is standard practice for life and performance coaches. As a performance coach, my approach to shifting mindset is ever-evolving. New levels of understanding are constantly revealed, pushing my methodology beyond conventional standards. Though my coaching career began as a mission to get what I want out of life, my destiny was to uncover a process for creating my own reality, feeling the way I want to feel, and passing that knowledge on to others. I'm honored to share my journey with you and, I hope, empower you to do the same.

Over the past year of my life, a series of breakthroughs has given me a level of success that was once impossible. While I have done the impossible, this ability is not uniquely mine. Potential for greatness lies within all of us. I have simply discovered a new way to move beyond limitations of the past. By approaching the present from this new perspective, you can access a clearer view of the big picture. That basic process is how you do the impossible and crush any target.

Think about doing the impossible as exploring your full potential. I constantly remind my clients (and myself): *You decide the primary focus of your life*. I suggest making the exploration of your full potential your primary focus. Explore yourself, your relationships, and your interests. Exploring your full potential is a decision. When you make the conscious decision to lean into the exciting challenges life presents, greatness will become your reality, and life will be a lot more fun.

Let's enter the boundless universe of performing at our highest level. Let's break the chains of the standard and the conventional. Let's recognize every moment as potentially life changing by shaping our own reality. Your journey to doing the impossible has begun. Your job is to embrace the path and keep moving forward.

WHAT IS THE IMPOSSIBLE?

Conventional interpretations of *the impossible* paint it as unattainable, intimidating, and unreasonable. Conjuring thoughts of something mystical that only heroes conquer, the impossible can elicit fear and inadequacy. From this perspective, the impossible *seems* insurmountable and therefore it is. Accepting something as beyond our capability immediately limits our potential. By redefining the impossible, we can fundamentally expand the realm of possibility.

My life experience has reshaped my view of the impossible. Today I see the impossible simply as an uncommon target. Knowing that it is as achievable as any other target, I see that the impossible has become exhilarating as opposed to unattainable, inspiring instead of intimidating, and aspirational not unreasonable. Believing the impossible is unattainable holds it out of reach. Redefining the impossible makes it accessible.

Think of someone who has crushed perceived limits on human potential. Undoubtedly, that person believed they were capable of expanding human potential, no matter what other people thought or said about it. They believed it was possible, and so it was.

What is the key to achieving that level of success? The answer is beliefs. Consciously or subconsciously, we often categorize ambitious goals as impossible, blocking greatness. We *believe* we are limited, which automatically limits our potential. We discount a target as impossible, instead of seeing it for what it is— just a target. Sure, it may be unconventional, and others may see it as illogical or unreasonable, but an uncommon target is just a target.

To mark the beginning of your transformation, I encourage you to redefine the impossible immediately. From this moment on, *the impossible is just an uncommon target.*

Let's get into alignment. Answer these questions:
- Do you understand that the impossible is just an uncommon target?
- Are you ready to move into alignment with hitting impossible targets?
- Are you ready to explore more personal growth and breakthroughs than ever before?

Now let's integrate.

Repeat After Me (out loud):
- *I take full ownership of my life and everything in it.*
- *I take full ownership of my past, present, and future.*
- *I understand that the size of a target is irrelevant because an impossible target is just an uncommon target.*
- *I understand that I can aim at any target I want, regardless of what other people think.*
- *I understand that the only person who will ever really understand my impossible target is me.*

Frame-Shifting Exercise

Imagine for a moment that you have decided to do the impossible and you have hit your first impossible target.

- Can you get a sense of a future version of you that has hit an impossible target?
- Can you imagine a version of you in the future that knows you can hit impossible targets?
- Can you get a sense of a future version of you that finds joy in life from knowing you can have anything that you want?

Great. Hold your awareness on that version of you for ten seconds. How do you feel now?

WHY DO THE IMPOSSIBLE?

Satisfaction in life comes from the experience. We've been conditioned to chase the result.

That is a great question. Why should you do the impossible?

Achievement is mistakenly considered the source of professional and personal satisfaction. Simply becoming successful is not the right reason for doing the impossible. Success is not our ultimate purpose. We exist to grow, expand, and share our passion with the world. While our aligned existence is the breeding ground for success, many people don't make the distinction between purpose and achievement. Mistakenly we create expectations for what life will become once we reach a certain success milestone, thinking that then our worth will be validated and our efforts celebrated. We think, *Once this happens, I can truly enjoy life*. Unknowingly, we hold these beliefs on an unstable pedestal that positions us to ignore the joy of the journey.

Doing the impossible is not about the achievement or the end result. It is not about proving our worth through the amount of money in a bank account or the number of properties purchased. Accepting the challenge of being exceptional is deciding to experience the exhilaration of leaving our comfort zone and actively pursuing expansion.

Expansion leads to inspired ideas and strategies that enhance earning power and capability. Many people seek performance coaching to increase income, but making more money is not their true target (whether they know it or not). Freedom, time, and authority are the real targets. Money is just a resource that can supply freedom, time, and authority, and make it easier to live life on our own terms. Money is only the means to our actual target—more choices and opportunities. Just as success is merely a by-product of accessing our inherent greatness.

Misinterpretation of the true source of fulfillment takes us out of the present and leads to living in the future. Delaying joy until you reach an arbitrary level of success is no way to live. Waiting until the right number of zeroes appears on our paycheck diminishes the value, excitement, and power of our unique path. After wasting years living in the future, I realized that pursuing my passion wholeheartedly is exponentially more satisfying than achieving a certain target or making a certain amount of money.

Do the impossible because you want to heighten your experience of life. Do the impossible because playing full out is an amazing feeling. Do the impossible because it will have a positive impact on the world. Validate your own worth by making the most of your time on this planet. Celebrate your own existence by engaging with life beyond limitations. Liberate yourself from working for future enjoyment by savoring the process of life today and every day.

Do the impossible because you want to maximize your time. You are already putting in the hours necessary for achieving greatness. How many days a week do you work? How many hours a day? Whatever your numbers are, there are people putting in the same amount of work and getting exceptional, unprecedented results. Doing the impossible is undoubtably more challenging than settling for average, but it is not necessarily more time-consuming.

In this moment, commit to the awe-inspiring challenge of doing the impossible. Commit to validating and celebrating yourself. Commit to maximizing the time you already spend working. Commit to taking on the impossible because you want more choices and opportunities. Most important, commit to being present for the journey because it's the best part.

Let's get into alignment. Answer these questions:
- Are you ready to do the impossible?
- Are you ready for a fulfilling, exciting journey exploring your full potential?
- Are you ready to walk the path to the impossible?

Excellent. Now let's integrate.

Repeat After Me (out loud):
- *I take full ownership of my life and everything in it.*
- *I take full ownership of my past, present, and future.*
- *From this moment on, I choose to explore the mindset of doing the impossible.*
- *From this moment on, I choose to live in a reality where doing the impossible is just a normal thing I do.*
- *I enjoy exploring the unknown and doing amazing things.*
- *I love doing the impossible because the results are amazing.*
- *I easily find resources to help me do the impossible.*
- *I choose to believe this 100 percent, past, present, and future—all versions of me. And I immediately take ownership of anything contradictory to this and integrate all of it now.*

Frame-Shifting Exercise
- Can you get a sense of a future version of you that loves doing amazing things?
- Can you imagine a version of you in the future that lives in the mindset of possibility and expansion?

- Can you get a sense of a future version of you that inspires others to do impossible things?
- Can you get a sense of a future version of you that always finds the resources you need?
- Can you get a sense of a future version of you that has mastered frame shifting?

Great. Hold your awareness on that version of you for ten seconds. How do you feel now?

WHY DON'T MORE PEOPLE DO THE IMPOSSIBLE?

Looming in our subconscious, the threat of failure often keeps us tethered to our comfort zone. The pain of failing can be excruciating, debilitating, and even unbearable. Once we've experienced it, our natural human response is to avoid taking that risk. Wired in our physiological and neurological systems, the mammalian response to risk is stress. Designed for survival, we avoid failure because we know it could harm us. Stress indicates vulnerability, which is uncomfortable and conventionally undesirable. While we cannot completely eliminate risk, pain, or stress, we can shift our perspective to see them as indicators as opposed to liabilities.

Being vulnerable to failure can be stressful and painful. This is one reason more people aren't doing the impossible. Though it is a normal, completely understandable response, viewing failure as a negative experience ignores the big picture. Failure makes us stronger, stretches us, and encourages growth. Our journey makes us who we are meant to be, failures and all. Nothing is learned by hitting the ball every time you swing the bat.

Have you ever focused on a target and failed? Of course you have. It's an unavoidable part of the human journey. How did that failure feel? Maybe it felt so bad you decided to avoid going through that experience ever again. Overcoming the fear of failure is one of the biggest challenges of doing the impossible. Fear of failure can't be completely avoided because it originates in our DNA. Nonetheless, this aspect of being human should not stop us from meeting our full potential. We are wired to avoid pain and discomfort, but we were born to be great.

Another reason people remain in their comfort zone, never attempting the impossible, is because they have been successful in their comfort zone. Using the same strategies to get a reliable result seems appealing on the surface. Once we dig a little deeper, though, we find that settling for the same level of success results in stagnation. Relying exclusively on previously verified actions limits potential and possibility, meaning that past success can directly hinder future success when we avoid expansion and growth. Staying in our comfort zone, even if we are successful there, limits what we achieve, earn, and experience. Placing more value on the certainty of the same old success than on the power of transformational growth, many people are ignoring their full potential and may not even know it.

Striving to hit a target outside our experience is typically uncomfortable. While there is a small percentage of the population that thrives on the excitement of the unknown, it's not natural to all of us. Admittedly, my natural instinct is not that of the rare achievement thrill seeker. As with most people, my life had to push me toward the fear of failure, and actual failure, so I could conquer it. Failure brings growth by giving us the opportunity to survive it. Failure helps us realize that the fear of missing the target is often worse than the pain of falling short. Today I embrace the excitement of going big and thriving beyond my comfort zone by putting fear of failure in its proper place. By operating from a mindset in which failure is an essential part of our journey, not a catastrophe, we can reduce the fear around it and more easily learn the lessons life is sending us.

One of the most mind-boggling reasons more people aren't doing the impossible is their resistance to obtaining the end result. Personal experience has revealed the inner workings of this strange, often unconscious, aversion to success and wealth. For years I struggled with accepting financial success. A valid question is, *Why would anyone resist success?* The best way I know to explain resistance to success is by sharing part of my story.

When I was in fourth grade, we moved to a prosperous area called Diamond Bar, California. My parents both worked so we could afford to live there, but things were tight. It became clear to me that we were not as wealthy as our neighbors.

Growing up I consistently heard, "We can't afford it." So, I started telling myself, *I can't afford it.* That perspective became ingrained in my brain and had lasting effects. From a young age, my financial identity was based in scarcity rather than abundance. Into my teens, I found that negative emotions and thoughts continued to develop around money and wealth, which took me decades to fully understand.

When half of my classmates got new BMWs for their sixteenth birthdays, I got my first job. It was at the Diamond Bar Golf Course during the summer between my freshman and sophomore year. At the end of the summer, something happened that further defined my relationship with money. Though I understand it now, it was a long road to realizing the effect it had on me and how I carried that moment from the past into my present.

After working all summer at the golf course, I had saved $700, which was quite a chunk of money back then. I was only making $4.25 an hour, but without many expenses, almost all my money went straight into a bank account. Since I was a minor, I couldn't have an account of my own, so my account was connected to my parents' bank account. One day, I went to the bank to check my account expecting to see $700, and my balance was $0.

I didn't know what had happened. I went home and told my mom my account was empty. She said, "Yeah, I know. I borrowed it to buy groceries." Without asking me, my mom had taken all of my summer earnings. Even though she replaced the money in a few days, that experience created a belief. The belief was: If I save money... it will be taken.

At that moment, I stopped saving money. When I had money, I spent it, subconsciously believing it would be taken. It was not that long ago that I still had a resistance to saving money and often found myself arguing with my wife about it. During those arguments, I still couldn't see that my resistance to saving money was rooted in a misguided belief created by one experience.

Another layer of my negative financial identity was based on the fact that no one in my family ever made a lot of money. It seemed impossible and wrong to reach a level of financial success outside of my family's social norm. Subconsciously, I was afraid that my family wouldn't love me anymore if I became wealthy.

As an adult, I had beliefs I had adopted as a child and teen that defined my relationship with money and success, hindering my performance. My perspective around money and wealthy people was stuck. Without even knowing it, I was living in a self-perpetuating cycle of financial sabotage. In retrospect, the patterns are easy to recognize. But at the time, I lacked the ability to see the big picture.

After three years in college studying civil engineering, I was 21 years old and still a freshman. Uninspired by school, I spent most of my time partying. Realizing I was wasting my time, I dropped out and moved to Northern California to start a career in technology sales. For the next sixteen years, I flourished in that industry. I produced above average profits and was highly regarded by my peers and colleagues. Occasionally, I would get bored, but I was making $120,000 a year and enjoying professional success.

Through a referral from a colleague, a job opportunity came up with another tech company. When I arrived for the interview, the regional hiring director introduced me to the staff as if I were a new hire, leading me to believe the job was in the bag.

When we sat down for the interview, he started by telling me the job came with a $200,000 annual salary. Part of me was ecstatic, while another part of me was terrified.

Prior to that day, my hiring record was exceptional. With a successful track record in tech sales and a history of getting 98 percent of the jobs I had ever applied for, I was perfectly prepared to nail the interview and land the job. But once he said $200,000 a year, I proceeded to have the worst interview of my life. It went so poorly that he didn't even call to let me know they went with another candidate.

At the time, I was baffled. It wasn't until ten years later after I started coaching that I realized why I had done so poorly. Because the position was beyond my financial comfort zone, I subconsciously sabotaged the opportunity. My belief that it would be wrong to exceed my family's financial standard blocked me from securing the job.

Years after that interview, I got a job making $200,000 a year. After only three months, I repeated my pattern of sabotage by losing the job. Once again, my resistance to financial success limited my potential.

My limited financial identity continued to plague me, even when I began to follow my passion for having my own business and dedicating years to improving my performance. At some level I was still holding to those misguided beliefs: *I can't afford it. If I save money...it will be taken. If I'm wealthy, my family won't love me.*

Before I started Jason Drees Coaching, I founded a series of start-ups, each of which were doomed to fail because of my resistance to having success and wealth. Even after I realized the source and depth of my misaligned financial mindset, I continued to repeat the same behavior. Understanding where my boundaries originated was not enough to break through my financial limits. My beliefs were still blocking the very thing I was trying to accomplish.

Often without even knowing it, I spent most of my life operating from a limited financial mindset. Expanding my earning power and maximizing my ability to accrue wealth was an impossibility until I changed my relationship with money. Trapped in a cycle, I had to discover how life really works in order to break free. Fortunately, now that I see the big picture and understand how life really works, I can help others remove resistance to doing the impossible.

I share that part of my journey to illustrate how we hold beliefs, often unknowingly, that affect our performance and limit possibility. Unraveling the complicated nature of limiting identity beliefs can seem daunting. But I have amazing news. You don't have to spend decades hitting a wall as I did. This book is designed to remove resistance and align you with who you really are with quickness and ease. You can move beyond any limiting identities without spending time focusing on the beliefs that created them. All you have to do is follow the instructions laid out in this book and stay ready and willing to take action. Becoming a person who does the impossible truly is that simple.

Doing the impossible will inevitably change you. Who you are right now is irrelevant. Who you will become on your journey to greatness is what matters. For that level of transformational growth, you must allow life to bring you necessary experiences, including failure. Sometimes a valuable lesson requires missing the target.

REQUIREMENTS FOR DOING THE IMPOSSIBLE

The requirements for doing the impossible encourage the engagement and understanding necessary for achieving accelerated, transformational growth with ease and flow. Life is built to push us toward our highest and greatest self through growth and expansion. Embracing life's design makes it more enjoyable, profitable, and fulfilling. The way you approach the present moment informs and determines the trajectory of your path and the level of your success.

The first requirement for doing the impossible is **you must be engaged in the game**. Simply reading this book will not transform you. Action is the most important component of doing the impossible. Understanding and analyzing the process will not expand your opportunities and choices. Manifestation does not make the impossible possible. Purposeful action is required.

Let's look at it this way: If you play basketball consistently, you will eventually take an elbow to the face. No one wants to endure that pain, but the only way to avoid it is to never play. You will never win if you don't play. Don't let the fear of getting elbowed (failure) stop you from getting in the game.

The next requirement for doing the impossible is **you must be willing to accept the path life is giving you**. Trusting the process of life aligns you with a reality where life is working for you, not against you. Believing life is out to get you makes that your experience of life.

The final requirement for doing the impossible is **you must follow the action**. The process of life does not follow a straight line. Sometimes an action seems disconnected from our target when it is actually a vital part of our path.

For example, imagine you wanted to quit your day job and you believe that becoming a real estate investor is your ticket. You start listening to the *BiggerPockets Podcast* and following Brandon Turner on social media. Brandon Turner leads you to discovering Jason Drees Coaching. You join the Jason Drees Coaching Mindset Academy community. After taking action in the program and shifting your mindset, you realize you don't enjoy real estate and you decide to follow your real passion. Following your passion leads to financial success, and you quit your job. Exploring real estate investing was crucial to deciding to follow your passion, which allowed you to quit your job. Even though the first steps you took may not have seemed aligned with your goal, by taking action you got in the game and life revealed your true path.

Sometimes an action may seem like a misstep when it's actually a starting point. If the version of you from the story hadn't initially pursued real estate, you might not have unlocked your true passion. The key is to keep moving forward by following the next action. Connections, choices, and opportunities appear when we are in the game, accepting our path, and following the action.

Understanding and meeting these requirements brings active engagement in your growth and expansion, which accelerates the process enabling radical transformation. Seeking radical transformation may seem scary, but it is important to remember that fear is not a warning sign to stay away. Fear is in our lives to be faced and conquered. Challenges are put in our path to bring new information and experiences. Embrace all of your path—the ups and downs, the starts and stops—and life will start unfolding for your highest and greatest good at an accelerated rate. The process of life will make you the person you are destined to become if you are taking the action. Fear, pain, and failure are unavoidable and necessary for achieving our destiny. By shifting our mindset and putting it in its proper place, we can use the messages it brings to crush any target.

Let's get into alignment. Answer these questions:
- Are you ready to put your comfort zone aside and live in the realm of greatness?
- Are you willing to be uncomfortable as you grow to do the impossible?
- Are you ready to follow the process of life in order to do the impossible?
- Are you ready to embrace failure as part of the path to doing the impossible?

- Are you ready to be an example to others for exploring your full potential?

Now let's integrate.

Repeat After Me (out loud):

- *I take full ownership of my life and everything in it.*
- *I take full ownership of my past, present, and future—all versions of me.*
- *I choose to be fully engaged in my life.*
- *I am willing to follow the path that life is giving me.*
- *I am willing to take the action that life presents to me.*
- *I look for naturally inspired action and am aware of when I feel resistance from forced, out-of-alignment action.*
- *I understand that failure is part of the process of life.*
- *I do not fear failure, because it is part of the process of life.*
- *I do my best to avoid failure and when it does occur, I embrace it as a learning opportunity.*
- *From this moment on, I choose to live in a reality where I see success and failure as part of the process of life.*
- *I choose to believe this 100 percent, past, present, and future—all versions of me. And I immediately take ownership of anything contradictory to this and integrate all of it now.*

Frame-Shifting Exercise

- Can you get a sense of the future version of you that is fully engaged in life?
- Can you imagine a version of you in the future that loves following your path in life?
- Can you get a sense of a future version of you that loves studying life in the process of it?

- Can you get a sense of a future version of you that embraces failure as a learning experience?
- Can you get a sense of a future version of you that embraces failure because you can see failure for what it is: preparation for doing the next important impossible thing?
- Can you get a sense of a future version of you that already knows all of this?

=

Great. Hold your awareness on that version of you for ten seconds. How do you feel now?

Chapter Three

REPEAT AFTER ME TO SHIFT YOUR MINDSET

The tools in this book are based on the one-on-one coaching practices I've developed over the past decade. The primary tools are the *Repeat After Me* recitations and the Frame-Shifting Exercises you've already been doing in the first two chapters of this book.

After years of coaching and countless hours spent addressing limiting beliefs one by one over multiple sessions with clients, I had a massive breakthrough regarding changing beliefs. I discovered it was possible to change a belief in minutes by simply taking ownership of what was causing resistance and avoidance to growth and expansion. The phrase "Repeat After Me" is the best way I have found to shift mindset and move quickly into the solution, as opposed to spending more time concentrating on limitations.

As I share higher-level concepts, we will use *Repeat After Me* to get into alignment with the material and release anything blocking transformation.

The phrase *Repeat After Me* is to be said out loud. Saying an intention aloud activates an idea, making it a reality.

Now let's integrate.

Repeat After Me (out loud):

- *I take full ownership of my life and everything in it.*
- *I take full ownership of my past, present, and future.*
- *I choose to explore the concept that reshaping my mindset reshapes my reality.*
- *I choose to allow incredible breakthroughs in my life.*
- *I choose to allow myself to easily explore new ideas and concepts.*
- *I choose to allow myself to easily release anything that is no longer in alignment with what I now know.*
- *I choose to easily explore the concepts in this book.*
- *I understand that Repeat After Me statements are a powerful tool to reshape my mindset.*
- *I allow Repeat After Me statements to work and transform my mindset even if I don't fully understand them, because I know that I can only accept something that is in alignment with what I believe.*
- *I allow myself to explore the full transformational potential in this book with an ease I've never experienced before.*
- *I allow myself to grow and transform with ease.*
- *From this moment on, I choose to live in a reality where growth and transformation are easy, fun, and rewarding.*
- *I choose to believe this 100 percent, past, present, and future—all versions of me. And I immediately take ownership of anything contradictory to this and integrate all of it now.*

Previously I believed transformation required time for learning and integration. Now I know change can happen instantly when I align my mindset with creating immediate change. Let's explore the space of immediate transformation and integration.

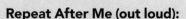

Repeat After Me (out loud):

- *I take full ownership of my life and everything in it.*
- *I take full ownership of my past, present, and future.*
- *From this moment on, I choose to live in a world of immediate transformation.*
- *So, I can immediately grow and transform whenever I want to.*
- *I no longer require additional effort, focus, or work to integrate change or transformation. I understand that anything can happen next.*
- *I understand that immediate change and integration is possible because in my life I have created immediate change and transformation on many occasions.*
- *I choose to live in a reality where this happens all the time.*
- *I choose to understand that this is possible.*
- *I choose to understand that I can grow as fast as I want to without pain or struggle.*
- *I choose to understand that it is possible for growth to be easy, fun, and exciting.*
- *I choose to live in a reality where radical, accelerated 10X growth is the norm and is accessible to me anytime I want it to be.*
- *I allow myself to fully receive accelerated success in my life.*
- *I take full ownership of anything contradictory to this, and I release it all now.*
- *I choose to believe this 100 percent, past, present, and future—all versions of me. And I immediately take ownership of anything contradictory to this and integrate all of it now.*

Frame-Shifting Exercise

- Can you get a sense of a future version of you that got something amazing out of this book?
- Can you imagine a version of you in the future that gets something amazing out of this book every time you read it?
- Can you get a sense of a future version of you that lives in a world of unlimited possibility in success?

- Can you get a sense of the future version of you that has created a life of success, connection, and wonder, and remembers that it all accelerated on this day?

Great. Hold your awareness on that version of you for ten seconds. How do you feel now?

PART TWO

THE FOUNDATION

Chapter Four

YOU, THE INFINITE BEING

Most people don't know how life really works.

As human beings, we desperately want to understand life. We strive to figure it out and when we can't find the winning equation, we often substitute lack of understanding with working ourselves to the point of exhaustion or copying other people. *The process* illustrates how life really works and reveals the power of your unique path and your internal guidance system, both of which will serve you far better than mimicking others or sacrificing your health and peace of mind for work.

If asked how to create success, most people will share the habits they used in *their* reality on *their* path to success. But the truth is, most likely, their success came from factors outside of their control. It wasn't their specific habits that created success. Life simply started going their way. Deals started closing. Leads started showing up. Magic started happening. Basically, life started to work for them in a way they desired.

No single success formula or model will work for everyone. At times, modeling others is an effective strategy. Following an established formula to make a real estate deal or flip a house can save time. Exploring the experience and expertise of successful people can have great value. But modeling other people doesn't always work, because *your* path to success is distinctly *yours*.

HUMAN POTENTIAL IS INFINITE

What is the potential of a human being? It continues to expand. Take the story of Roger Bannister and the four-minute mile. Prior to 1952, no one thought running a mile in four minutes was possible until Roger Bannister did it—expanding human potential. Bannister's record stood for just forty-six days, and runners have lowered the record seventeen times since his fateful run. Yet we still remember Bannister's name for his incredible breakthrough. He achieved the impossible; the others were just following in his (very fast) footsteps.

Human potential is infinite, making your potential infinite. As an infinite being, you are "subject to no limitation or external determination" (according to *Merriam-Webster*). Beyond limitation, you are brimming with untapped capability, free from constraints. Given enough time and dedication, you are capable of learning how to do anything. You are built for expanding human potential.

Let's get into alignment. Answer these questions:
- Do you understand there is no limit to what you can learn?
- Do you understand that there's no limit to what you can do?
- Are you ready to explore the concept of being an infinite being?

Now let's integrate.

Repeat After Me (out loud):

- *I take full ownership of my life and everything in it.*
- *I take full ownership of my past, present, and future.*
- *I choose to explore the concept of being an infinite being.*
- *I choose to explore my infinite nature.*
- *I hereby release anything that is preventing me from exploring my infinite nature.*
- *From this moment on, I choose to live in a reality where exploring my infinite nature happens automatically with ease.*
- *I accept and embrace all of my skills.*
- *I embrace and accept all of my gifts, known and unknown.*
- *I choose to believe this 100 percent, past, present, and future—all versions of me. And I immediately take ownership of anything contradictory to this and integrate all of it now.*

Frame-Shifting Exercise

- Can you get a sense of a future version of you that understands you are an infinite being?
- Can you imagine a version of you in the future that is connected to your infinite nature?
- Can you get a sense of a future version of you that understands and utilizes your unlimited capacity for growth and learning?
- Can you get a sense of a future version of you that helps other people remember their infinite nature?
- Can you get a sense of the future version of you that impacts the world by being who you are?

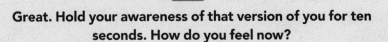

Great. Hold your awareness of that version of you for ten seconds. How do you feel now?

YOU ARE AN INFINITE BEING

From a spiritual point of view, have you wondered if we are more than these bodies we inhabit? Though spirituality is not the focus of this book, I've witnessed a recent movement in human consciousness toward a greater understanding of the part of us that is eternal. Exploration of spirituality profoundly impacted my personal growth and professional success. Sharing my discovery of the process without touching on this subject would neglect a vital part of my journey that helped me embrace and understand my infinite nature.

Have you ever looked in the mirror, regardless of how old you are, and recognized a part of you that never seems to age? I experience this feeling quite often. After almost five decades on the planet, when I look in the mirror, there is a part of me that feels timeless. I see that awareness as the part of me that is eternal.

When I was growing up, my family was not religious. We went to church sporadically for Easter or Christmas, but for the most part, we didn't participate in organized religion. Honestly, I hadn't thought much about it until I was in my late 20s when a series of events led me to investigate that corner of existence.

In 2005, my 21-year-old cousin Adam was killed in a drunk-driving accident. While trying to make sense of the loss of Adam, I started questioning life. Indications and synchronicities that life might hold more than I had previously believed entered my consciousness. I watched a show called *What Happens When We Die?* The timing of coming across that show was divinely curious, which further piqued my interest. Then I read the book *Journey of Souls* by Michael Newton, which gave me the perspective that maybe we are more than these bodies.

The year after Adam passed away, I went to a psychic, which I had never done before. As I sat with the psychic, a Hispanic woman in her 30s, she began to take on the cadence and mannerisms of Adam. It was strange because she sounded like a white kid in his 20s from Orange County, California. Adam had unique mannerisms and high energy. Watching a woman who had never met Adam talk and act like him showed me how much I didn't know. That day I realized I wanted and needed to explore the parts of existence beyond what we can see—beyond these bodies.

Though I had yet to spend much time thinking about spirituality, I always had a sense of my intuitive nature. Realizations and resources showed up in my life, often right on time. Sometimes it was the clarity I was looking for, and other times it was insight I didn't even know I needed. My life holds true to the clichéd theosophical statement, "When the student is ready, the teacher will appear." When I've needed guidance, the lessons and teachers who matched that moment showed up. It continues to amaze me. At the same time, it happens so often that sometimes I don't even realize it. Look back on your life. Can you pinpoint moments when what you needed arrived right on time, as if summoned by something beyond you?

After the experience with the psychic, I knew I had a decision to make. I could dismiss all the new information I had recently received, or I could explore my rising curiosity. If I brushed it off, I would stay in the same place. If I chose to explore this curiosity, it might lead to a different, deeper understanding of life. I could do nothing and continue to confirm what I already knew. Or I could align myself with growth and expansion. The decision was clear. I needed to experiment in the unknown. Now, with the advantage of hindsight, I see this as the start of my journey to becoming a coach.

Opening myself up to that part of existence was pivotal to finding my destiny—discovering a way of life that gives me all I ever wanted. Success and money, yes. But, most important, it has given me the tools to feel the way I want to feel and the ability to share the process with others.

In case you are struggling with the idea that you are an infinite being, let's go back to seventh grade science class. Do you remember learning about atoms? Atoms are like little planets made of neutrons, protons, and electrons. Do you remember what percentage of an atom is solid? An atom is 99.9999 percent empty space, which means the percentage of our universe that is physical is 0.0001 percent.

Stay with me now—that empty space is made of electrons that can only be accurately measured using quantum physics theory. The state of an electron is determined by the type of energy it is absorbing or reacting to at the moment of measurement. I don't pretend to understand quantum physics, but this tells me that I'm almost entirely made up of pure energy. And so are you.

The vibrational frequency of your atoms—your mindset—impacts, informs, and defines the reality you experience. If you are an infinite being made almost entirely of pure energy, doesn't it make sense that life will react to your vibrational frequency? After exploring this concept for the past decade, I admit I don't know exactly how it works. But I am certain it works because of the results I've seen in my life and the lives of my clients. Understanding it completely seems less important than being grateful for the ability to shape my reality and show others how to transform their experience of life.

As an infinite being, your default is a state of abundance. You live in a world of unlimited opportunity. Many of us believe, due to upbringing and socially conditioning, that we are born into a state of scarcity. We are taught to believe that if we work hard, we *might* be able to move into a state of abundance. Shifting into a state of abundance is as simple as recognizing you are already there and have always been there.

As a coach, I don't help people create success. How can I help an infinite being whose default is a state of abundance create success? I can't. I simply help people remove resistance to their natural default state of success.

Most of the people I coach are initially completely unaware of their full potential. They don't know anything about alignment or creating success through any method other than hard work. They don't know they are in misalignment with their default state of abundance. My role is to help people align themselves with what they want (their target) by tapping into their inherent power (their infinite nature).

By connecting with the part of them that is eternal—the part beyond their body—they begin expanding their potential, and success becomes a state of being rather than a goal. I have learned through my life experience and the results I've watched clients achieve that when you are aligned with your target, you will hit it. It's that simple. But the first step is understanding and embracing your infinite nature.

Let's connect to your infinite nature with this exercise.

- Put your attention on your body. Take all of your attention and put it on your body and nowhere else.
- Hold that attention as easily as you can. Hold it there for three breaths.
- Release that attention and move your attention to everything outside of your body.
- Hold that attention as easily as you can. Hold it there for three breaths.
- Put your attention on the center of your awareness inside of you, where you perceive everything from.
- Hold it there for three breaths.
- Let your attention begin to expand outward in all directions, as easily as you can.
- Let it expand past your room, past your house, past your city, past your state.
- Let your attention expand to include all of planet Earth.
- Hold it there for three breaths.
- Let your attention expand again until it includes the entire solar system.

- Hold it there for three breaths.
- Let your attention expand again until it includes all of the Milky Way galaxy.
- Let it keep expanding until it includes everything.
- Hold it there for ten breaths.
- Get a sense of where you come from.
- Connect with your infinite nature.

Now let's integrate.

Repeat After Me (out loud):

- *I take full ownership of my life and everything in it.*
- *I take full ownership of my past, present, and future.*
- *From this moment on, I choose to always remember my infinite nature.*
- *I choose to explore my full potential as an infinite being on this planet in this body now.*
- *I take full ownership of anything that is in contradiction to my new understanding of who I really am, an infinite being. And I release all of that now.*
- *I take full ownership of everything I've forgotten about who I really am. I remember it all now.*
- *I choose to explore life as an infinite being, spreading my positive impact to transform this world.*
- *I accept my role in the world as a contributing infinite being, among other infinite beings.*
- *I choose to experience rapid, accelerated growth and success in my life as an infinite being.*
- *I want to explore all of it now.*
- *I choose to believe this 100 percent, past, present, and future—all versions of me. And I immediately take ownership of anything contradictory to this and integrate all of it now.*

Frame-Shifting Exercise

- Can you get a sense of a future version of you that is always connected to your infinite nature?
- Can you get a sense of a future version of you that leverages your infinite nature to make a powerful, positive impact on the world?
- Can you imagine a version of you in the future that has been living with this truth for ten years?
- Can you imagine a future version of you that is even more unlimited than you are now?
- Hold that awareness on a future version for ten seconds.
- Can you imagine a future version of you that is even more unlimited than this one?

**Hold your awareness on that version of you for ten seconds.
How do you feel now?**

Chapter Five
MINDSET BASICS

The most powerful way to create transformation in your life is by shifting your perspective. Your perspective is your mindset. Here is a story that illustrates the power of mindset.

Let's say you like to run. Your favorite race is the mile. When you compete, you typically come in around fifth place. You don't really care much about winning, because you enjoy running.

When you run a mile race, you normally wear blue shoes. One day you are putting on your blue shoes before a race, and the sole from one of the shoes falls off. Luckily, your friend is there, and he has an extra pair of shoes that just happen to be your size. He lends you the shoes, and you put them on without noticing that they are red.

You run the race and come in first place! Your friend is so excited about your victory he lets you keep the red shoes. Over the next few months, you continue to wear the red shoes and win every race you run. You start to believe the red shoes are the reason you are winning.

Inspired by your recent victories, you decide to compete more seriously and fly to another city to run in a big race. When you get off the plane, your checked bag is not there to meet you. The airline tells you it won't arrive until after the race is over.

On a hunt for red shoes, you frantically run around to every store in town, only to find they are selling just blue shoes. No matter how hard you try, you can't find red shoes. You settle and buy a pair of blue shoes.

How do you think you're going to feel lacing up those blue shoes before the race? How are you going to feel at the starting line without your red shoes? Will you feel doubt, nervousness, unease, and uncertainty simply because your shoes are the wrong color?

In this vignette, the red shoes represent an empowered mindset. When you are wearing the red shoes, you are aligned with winning. You are approaching the race from a place of success. The blue shoes represent a disempowered mindset. When you are stuck in blue shoes, negative emotions such as doubt and uncertainty arise, creating resistance to success.

Back to the story. You run the race in the blue shoes, and you lose. In planning for the next race, you have a choice. You can decide to train harder in blue shoes (stay in a disempowered mindset) and hope hard work will make you run faster. Or you can do what works—do what enabled you to win—and just put on the red shoes (shift to an empowered mindset).

Concerning physical achievement, practice and hard work are a requirement for success. You don't become a professional athlete unless you train and perfect your skills. But the same is not true in business. In business, success can come from anywhere, from any direction, at any time—*if you are open to it*. In business, anything is possible in the next moment with an empowered mindset.

WHAT IS MINDSET?

Essentially, your mindset is your perspective. Expectations, belief structure, and social conditioning converge to form your perspective. Created by upbringing and environment, mindset is the combination of all your experiences.

Mindset is how you view the world. Always running, your mindset is defined by what country you live in, where you went to school, what TV shows and news you watch, what podcasts you listen to, your failures and successes, your emotions and reactions to those failures and successes, and all the other endless contributing factors that create your identity. Consciously or unconsciously, you approach everything you encounter from a mindset.

Paradoxically, mindset is both elusive and ever present. How often are you consciously aware of your perspective? I'm guessing not very often, especially if this is your first time exploring mindset. Day-to-day, evaluating our perspective is not typically on the to-do list (although it should be). Despite dictating our actions, emotions, and results, too often we inadvertently accept the conditions of our mindset as innately predetermined and unchangeable, with no pushback.

Because mindset is informed by how you think and what you know, I like to think of it as the brain's operating system. Evolving and upgrading over time, this operating system produces increasingly better thoughts, ideas, and strategies as it gathers more information. New levels of understanding shift your mindset, expanding your potential and capability. Occurring naturally, experience and knowledge control the evolution of your mindset. To accelerate growth and expansion, you can intentionally shift your mindset, saving time usually spent learning by trial and error.

Remember, you are an infinite being with limitless potential. Consciously shifting to an empowered mindset can expedite success by engaging your full potential. The process begins by transforming your beliefs with purposeful intention.

BELIEFS

The more we let go of what we hold to be true, the more we allow what is possible, or seemingly impossible, to happen.

Your beliefs are your opinions based on life experience. We can also call them stories, justifications, or excuses. From your point of view, you might swear your beliefs are facts.

What is the difference between a fact and a belief? A fact is measurable by a third party. A belief is an acceptance of something as true. Holding a belief too tightly can make it seem unchangeable, but beliefs are not facts. Beliefs can be changed.

Truth is defined by perspective, meaning there are multiple truths depending on how you look at something. Take a cylinder for example. When you look at a cylinder from the top, it's a circle. When you look at a cylinder from the side, it can appear to be a square or a rectangle. Truth is variant. Perspective changes truth.

Loosening your grip on what you hold to be true is the first step to harnessing the power of mindset. Grasping on to the comfort of current beliefs, even when they hinder growth, limits anything outside of our established belief structure. To shift mindset and release greatness, you must be open to adopting new beliefs about yourself and how life works. Believing there is only one truth, and you already know it, blocks growth and expansion.

Your beliefs inform how you view and interact with the world (your mindset). When you align your beliefs with what you want and who you want to become, you are consciously aligning yourself with success. By taking ownership of your perspective and embracing new empowering beliefs, you can change your truth and alter your reality. Clutching old disempowering beliefs, though it may sometimes be comforting, limits your future perspective and effectively denies your infinite nature.

Not releasing deep-rooted beliefs is one of the biggest obstacles to success. *If you want to change your reality, you need to change your beliefs.*

HOW ARE BELIEFS CREATED?

Beliefs inform your understanding of how life works—not just of how life works in general but how life works specifically for you. Beliefs are created to give order to our world as we try to understand it.

Most of our beliefs are a product of social conditioning. Unwritten rules and requirements for success become imbedded in our brains based on our environment and social norms. Those restrictive conditions become beliefs that often limit our potential, blocking accelerated growth.

Beliefs are also created to justify past failures and previous success. For example, when you want to close a big deal and it doesn't happen, your brain gives you a reason why you weren't successful. Maybe a simple explanation like *I just didn't work hard enough* pops into your head. To understand your failure, you reinforce the belief that hard work is a requirement of success. When we hold a belief, we also accept the inverse as true. By believing hard work creates success, you inadvertently decide you won't be successful without working hard.

Approaching the next deal, your mindset is aligned with working hard, disconnecting yourself from what you really want. You don't want to work hard; you want success. Consciously aligning yourself with success is much more effective, and enjoyable, than focusing on working hard.

Beliefs based in the past can inadvertently limit your future. Disempowering beliefs, such as *I have to work hard to be successful*, place conditions on success and block possibility. You may currently believe that hard work is the key to success because you've had success after working hard. Holding this belief makes hard work a requirement for success. What if you adopted a new belief that removed this requirement? Try this one on for size: *Ultimate success is achieved with ease and flow.*

Operating from the past can feel safe. The past provides a level of certainty because the outcomes are known. But moving into a world of endless possibility requires creating certainty in the unknown. How do you create certainty in the unknown? By changing your beliefs about yourself and how life works for you. To move beyond your current beliefs about yourself—who you are and what you are capable of—you must shift your mindset to a future version of yourself, a version that is free from who you were and what you did in the past.

Maintaining beliefs based in reaction to past failure and success denies your full potential. To reach full potential and do the impossible, you must remove any perquisites your social conditioning and past experiences have instilled. Your beliefs about the past are your limitations of the future. This is so important that I want you to Repeat After Me: *My beliefs about the past are my limitations of the future.*

CHANGING BELIEFS AND WHY IT CAN SEEM HARD

During my own self-exploration, mastering my beliefs was a major challenge. As shown in my quest to shift my limited financial mindset, beliefs can be so deeply rooted that they become ingrained in our identity. For example, if you believe you are destined for success but identify yourself as unworthy of success, you are holding two contradictory beliefs. The reason changing beliefs can be hard is because most people don't know how to remove the contradictions.

Human beings believe something 100 percent or 0 percent. If you ever feel that you believe something between 0 percent and 100 percent, it means you are holding two beliefs in contradiction. It is our nature to hold contradictory ideas simultaneously, and it may not be beneficial to work in absolute terms concerning all beliefs. But when it comes to recognizing your full potential and infinite nature, I encourage you to remove any gray areas that are blocking inspiration and expansion. Knowing with 100 percent certainty that you are destined for greatness will expedite success and remove unnecessary struggle. In coaching, I help clients uncover their overlapping contradictory beliefs about who they are and what they are truly capable of accomplishing.

Conquering contradictory beliefs is nuanced, which makes it seem difficult. Doubt often arises when we try to validate a new belief because a secondary, contradictory belief still exists. Unable to embrace the new belief 100 percent, doubt becomes resistance to change.

Have you ever tried to change your beliefs? Maybe you read a book on the topic or went to a personal growth event. Many of my clients attempted to alter their belief structure prior to seeking coaching, and when it became a struggle, they gave up.

Determined to live life on my own terms and to feel the way I wanted to feel, I spent years trying to master my beliefs. From screaming at the top of my lungs and spending hours on daily incantations, to EFT tapping (a technique in which you tap key areas of your shoulders, neck, head, and face to release negative energy), I would try anything. In fact, the desire to master my beliefs was one of the reasons I became a coach. During all of these attempts, I knew deep down there had to be a faster, easier, better way to change beliefs. Last year, I discovered *framing* and it has revolutionized my life and the life of my clients.

Mastering beliefs by removing contradictions can be a hard concept to grasp and often even more difficult to implement. Revisiting the past to uproot disempowering beliefs is time-consuming and, oftentimes, painstaking. The beauty of my new technique—framing—is you don't have to spend more time in the past to move beyond it, and you don't have to understand how it works to reap the benefits.

Before framing, I would work with a client to uncover beliefs and follow negative emotions to the contradicting belief, changing each belief one at a time. Now that I understand framing, that process is unnecessary. Framing allows you to shift your beliefs without spending time on each individual belief, aligning you with the reality you want instantly.

Framing is so powerful I feel as if I've seen behind the curtain of how life really works. Since this discovery, my business has exploded, more resources have shown up right on time, my success has accelerated, and I live knowing that I'm unstoppable. Watching my clients experience the same radical growth and reclaim their freedom is beyond rewarding and validates the life-changing force of this discovery.

LIMITING BELIEFS

If you've studied personal growth, you may be familiar with the concept of *limiting beliefs*. Limiting beliefs are thoughts and opinions about ourselves and how life works based on past experience and social conditioning. Denying our infinite nature, causing negative emotional reactions, and creating resistance, limiting beliefs block growth and expansion.

For example, pretend you work in sales, and you need to make cold calls. Before you even pick up the phone, you feel negative emotions and resistance. Traditional coaching strategies would say your beliefs about cold calling are the reason you feel resistance to that action. Your beliefs about a specific action are limiting you, hence limiting beliefs. This is the way that I used to coach. This is the way most coaches teach. This is the old way.

The old way requires taking lower-level ownership of your life and seeking lower-level awareness of how to change your life. The action—cold calling—is what we usually focus on and try to change. Concentrating on limiting beliefs keeps you at the action or micro level.

The new way—framing—focuses on the macro level (frame). Framing goes beyond a specific action or subject. A limiting belief specifically about cold calling is only a symptom of a larger disconnect. Misalignment with the target (success) is the problem and the real source of resistance. Transforming our environment of operation (our frame) by reshaping or reframing our reality is the fastest and most effective way to change beliefs.

Again, my story serves as a great example. When I was working from a limited financial mindset, money triggered negative emotion. Having money was the target, but my mindset was not in alignment with having money. My negative emotions about money were on the micro level and not the real problem. Focusing on the macro level, misalignment with success was the true issue. The negative emotions were only indicators that I needed to shift my financial mindset by reframing my environment of operation. I had to change my beliefs about money (macro level) to remove resistance to the action needed to hit my target (micro level).

You will notice in this example that my negative emotions served as indicators. Here is a simple way to think about utilizing emotions as indicators. It is like when you are driving down the highway and you drift to the side of the road. You hit the grading marks, and your ride becomes bumpy. The bumps are not a problem. The bumps are just an indicator to steer your car back into alignment with the center of the road. Unfortunately, when it comes to changing beliefs, many approaches spend unnecessary time driving into negative emotions. Concentrating on limiting beliefs wastes time because we are trying to fix things that don't need to be fixed. The negative emotion shows you that your perspective is misaligned. That is what needs your attention.

Often, I find myself having the same conversation with many of my clients. They say, "If I was just confident, I could do (blank)." Or "If I just wasn't so scared..." or "If I just wasn't doubtful..." and so on. Confidence, fear, and doubt are not the problem. They are simply emotions telling you it's time to shift your approach. It's time to shift your perspective.

We have been socially conditioned to process negative emotions as cues that it's time to work hard, time to grind, time to hustle. This is a misguided, limiting belief. Emotions are important indicators that tell us our internal reality needs to shift. It's not time for hard work. It's time to release beliefs that no longer serve us. It's time to put on the red shoes. When you feel unconfident, afraid, and doubtful, life is telling you to take ownership of your beliefs and shift your perspective. Once you master this, shifting mindset will become as easy as changing your shoes.

I spent a lot of time coaching people on limiting beliefs because I didn't know any other way. Four years ago, it would have taken me six months to get a client to see a particular point of view that could immediately change their life. Today, I can get any client to see that point of view in less than an hour because of framing.

When you shift the frame, you shift the limiting beliefs. But the opposite is not true in every case. Shifting limiting beliefs does not automatically shift your frame. You may overcome the fear of cold calling while still operating in a frame of doubt. If a higher-level shift doesn't occur, that same doubt will keep you from taking other actions, which would then require more time and attention.

Here is the point: Conventional coaching methodologies have it backward. Focusing on changing a belief at the action level ignores your environment of operation (your frame). The environment you are operating in is actually what determines the result, not the limiting beliefs. Limiting beliefs reside at the action level, which is the lowest level of the process. I'm going to take you to a level of understanding that creates inspired action and removes the negative emotions that can so often leave us stagnant.

BEYOND LIMITING BELIEFS

Let's review. A major component of conventional mindset coaching is exposing and eradicating limiting beliefs. Many personal growth programs dedicate time and energy to uncovering, dissecting, and analyzing each limiting belief to achieve a mindset shift around one specific action. Framing flips that model upside down. This approach is more effective and efficient because it initiates a solution without hours spent on rehashing the problem.

Framing began to reveal itself in 2014 (though I wouldn't come to fully understand the process until late 2020). At that time, I was working at a leading coaching company. I'd figured out how to help people create radical mindset shifts, but it didn't work for every client.

On a few separate occasions, I found myself with two clients facing similar problems concerning disempowered financial mindset, which is one of the most common problems clients bring to coaching. While coaching the two clients, I used the same exact approach with each one, addressing their limiting beliefs and negative emotions around money. Though the same approach was used with both clients, their results were dramatically different. Over the next few months, one client would start making a lot more money while the other client's income level would stay the same.

Why did one client start to make more money and the other didn't when they both received the same coaching? To find the answer I had to go beyond limiting beliefs. Both clients addressed and changed their limiting beliefs around money. But the client that made more money experienced an additional evolution on a higher level. Having not yet discovered framing, I didn't know what to call that level of awareness at the time.

As discussed earlier, limiting beliefs occur at the micro level. When framing was revealed to me less than a year ago, I finally realized the reason those two clients achieved opposite results. The difference between the two experiences was at the macro level. The client that began to create success had gone beyond limiting beliefs and had shifted frames. The other client had only changed their limiting beliefs, and their frame was still misaligned with success.

Years after that experience, I realized how framing gives you a higher vantage point for shifting mindset and changing beliefs. This discovery radically altered my approach to life and coaching. I came to understand that limiting beliefs are irrelevant because we now have access to creating an empowered frame without spending time on what is creating inaction or misaligned action and move right into taking aligned, inspired action. I don't know why it is different now, but I know it is different. As human beings, we have access to higher levels of awareness, higher levels of consciousness, higher levels of ownership, and higher levels of potential. We have the ability to transform our lives at an accelerated pace. We are only beginning to discover how powerful we really are, and how much we create our own reality.

Let's get into alignment. Answer these questions:

- Are you ready to learn even more about how mindset works?
- Are you ready to be in control of your mindset?
- Are you ready to understand when your mindset is out of alignment?

Now let's integrate.

Repeat After Me (out loud):

- I take full ownership of my life and everything in it.
- I take full ownership of my past, present, and future.
- I understand that my mindset contains beliefs that are created from my life experience or from environmental, social conditioning.
- I understand that limiting beliefs are not a problem; they are simply an indicator of misalignment—between my mindset and the target I'm focused on.
- I choose to understand that it is easy to change beliefs when you know how to do it.
- The easiest way to change beliefs is by taking ownership of them.
- I understand that I can change my mindset and beliefs.
- I understand that I am in control of my mindset and beliefs.
- From this moment on, I choose to live in a reality where I automatically notice when I'm feeling out of alignment. Where I also always notice when my mindset and beliefs are out of alignment with what I want.
- I understand that this book is changing my mindset and beliefs.
- I understand that every time I read this book, I get something new out of it, and the more I read it, the more it will transform me.
- I understand that the tools in this book, like Repeat After Me mantras and frame shifting, are ways to shift my mindset.
- I choose to believe this 100 percent, past, present, and future—all versions of me. And I immediately take ownership of anything contradictory to this and integrate all of it now.

Frame-Shifting Exercise

- Can you get a sense of a future version of you that sees negative emotions as indicators of misalignment?
- Can you get a sense of a future version of you who knows that limit-

=

Great. Hold your awareness on this version of you for ten seconds. How do you feel now?

INTRODUCTION TO FRAMING

You can shift your mindset in seconds by shifting your frame.

During my quest for understanding how life works, I discovered what I call our *frame*. Prior to this point, I didn't fully comprehend how success was created, because I was operating with only two-thirds of the equation. When I uncovered this last piece, everything expanded.

Our frame creates our mindset, which guides our thoughts, ideas, motivations, and actions. The frame we hold around a specific subject or action is the starting point. When we construct our frame with elevated awareness, we achieve success faster than ever before. By aligning awareness—focus—with what we want, we can establish an environment of operation conducive to hitting our target. And not just hitting our target but doing it with ease and flow. Because when we start from a frame that is aligned with our target and that consciously works with what life brings us, we are led to inspired action.

Framing is the primary tool for doing the impossible. If you've been working through the exercises in this book, you've already shifted your frame several times. The simplest definition of framing is reshaping reality. There are three parts, or levels, within framing:

1. *Action*—You action is where you spend most of your time and energy. As humans, we are focused primarily on actions we need to take to get what we want out of life (money, job, success).
2. *Mindset*—Your mindset is your operating system. It creates your thoughts, ideas, emotions, motivation, and inspiration. Your mindset

determines how you perceive or view the subject. Strategy and action are determined by mindset.

3. *Frame*—Your frame is your consciousness or the awareness that is you. It is you as a being. It's all of you. Your frame is what interacts with life. It is what life responds to. It is your vibrational frequency, which you determine, consciously or unconsciously. It determines if you have a good day or a bad day. It determines if you keep operating on the same level or if you expand into doing the impossible. Frame determines mindset.

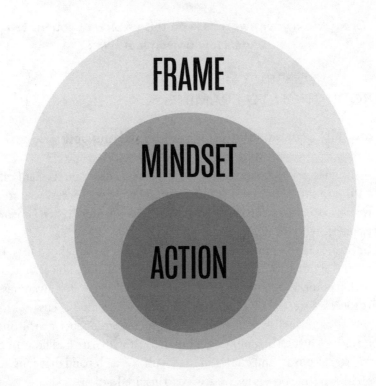

Your frame dictates your results through the process:
1. Frame creates mindset.
2. Mindset creates subject.
3. Action creates results.

Since this concept runs counter to conventional thinking, it can be difficult to understand initially. Logically, action alone creates results. From an elevated perspective, the process actually begins levels above action. Your frame creates your mindset, your mindset creates action, and your actions create results. Therefore, an aligned frame creates an aligned mindset, an aligned mindset creates aligned action, and aligned action creates the result you want. The opposite is also true. A misaligned frame creates a misaligned mindset, a misaligned mindset creates misaligned action, and misaligned action creates an undesirable result.

Your frame is your starting point, which is crucial to creating success. Amazingly, framing lets you choose your starting point, giving you the power to reshape reality.

Most people unconsciously live and operate within a frame determined by their past or present. Their mindset is stuck in reaction to their life as they currently understand it. Through the process of frame shifting, you can choose your reality by establishing a new starting point. Before taking any action, you align yourself with what you want from an elevated awareness. It's a subtle shift that makes a massive difference.

Frame your exploration of the process with the awareness of a future version of yourself that fully understands these concepts. Establish your starting point by selecting and implementing the belief that your infinite nature opens you up to unbounded possibility.

PART THREE

RESHAPING REALITY

Chapter Six
CREATING YOUR OWN REALITY

Are you living your life in reaction or in creation?

LIVING IN AN ATTRACTION-BASED UNIVERSE

Now that you know you are an infinite being with limitless potential and you have a base knowledge of beliefs, mindset, and frame, let's expand into the world of creating your own reality.

We live in an attraction-based universe, meaning like attracts like. Every moment of every day, you are creating your reality. Like a giant magnet, you are perpetually attracting your experience of life. The reality we experience is determined by our frequency. Aligning who you are (your frame) with what you want sets your energy at the frequency of your target.

Let's go back to seventh grade science class. You may remember learning that two particles, if unaffected by outside forces in space, are attracted to each other.

What does this mean? It means you attract what you are. This truth is at the core of what I love about life. If you are in frequency alignment with what you want, you will absolutely, 100 percent, get it every time.

You have a destiny. You have a unique path. How do you know if you are in alignment with your unique path? Intuition is your guide. Misalignment occurs when you get caught up in doing what you *think* you need to do instead of doing what you *know* you should do.

People spend years stuck in unfulfilling jobs hoping one day they will be able to follow their passion. I've been there, and odds are you have been there too, if only for a short time.

Let's pretend you know your destiny is to be the number one handbag designer in the world, but you believe you need financial independence to do it. By operating from a frame defined by that belief, you have inadvertently put destiny on hold. In reaction to social conditioning and/or past experience, you have made success conditional, blocking yourself from following your passion and aligning with your unique path. If you are passionate about making handbags, start making them now! Your passion is the part of you that knows how to get in alignment with your unique path.

When you are in alignment with your destiny, you attract that reality. In all areas of your life, professional and personal, your path will lead you in the direction of greatest growth. By setting the frequency of your frame to match your unique path, you can accelerate growth while experiencing life on your terms. When we shift our mindset to include empowering beliefs, the impossible becomes possible because we are coming from a place of creation instead of reaction.

If you are resisting any part of the path, you are resisting the end result.

ATTRACTION + ACTION

Some mindset methodologies are based on the law of attraction. From my perspective, the law of attraction implies you can sit under a tree and the things you desire will simply fall in your lap. That is not how life works. Attraction becomes connection through the process of life plus action. When you get into alignment with the process, life will bring you success and opportunities. But there is always a process, and there is always action.

As a performance coach, I frequently encounter people who are stuck in a cycle of inaction. The reasons for inaction are endless. Spending time considering what action to take and endlessly weighing options is a classic pitfall. Call it perfectionism or analysis paralysis, it's really just avoidance. *Procrastination* and *laziness* are other popular labels for avoidance. Regardless of what we call it, the solution is always to "get in the game" by taking action.

In my experience, behind all shades of inaction looms fear. Often it is that dreadful fear of failure we discussed earlier. Life is full of risk. Avoiding vulnerability through inaction will not eliminate risk. Resisting action is denying your destiny and avoiding your unique path.

KNOWN VS. UNKNOWN

You are an infinite being and so is everyone else. We are all infinite beings with overlapping realities. The only thing you can control is you and your reality. You can't control anyone else or the way they experience and create their reality.

We like to think we can control other people, but we can't. Our parents, our siblings, our colleagues, our friends, our partners, and even our children are infinite beings who cannot be controlled. We must allow others their own experiences and for them to chart a course down their own unique path. Trying to control them will only create stress and misalignment within us.

I refer to the things outside of our control as *the unknown*, which includes other people. Some of us would love to control the unknown. Many of us spend countless hours worrying because we can't control the unknown. You can't control the unknown, but you do have the ability to shape your reality and decide who and what take up space in your life.

What determines whether your new product launch is successful or a failure? What determines the people who come into our lives? We don't know. I was wasting time trying to control the unknown when I discovered that as an infinite being, I can shape what comes up in the unknown. The people and results that appear from the unknown are a match to who I am and the reality I create. Whether a new employee turns out to be a terrific resource or a poor hire, it is all based on my energy.

To expand how you think about and interact with the world and other people, you need to start to play in the realm of the unknown. You need to start to create certainty in the unknown. That's where the magic happens. When we live in uncertainty, we often try to control the future in a misguided attempt to acquire security. We have doubt and fear that something bad or negative is going to happen, so we try to control outcomes and waste time on false expectations.

Anything you can do in this moment to prevent something bad or negative from happening, you are most likely already doing. There is no need to fixate on preparing for the worst or predicting the details of the future. Your instinct is already moving you to take actions in an attempt to avoid trouble. You won't always be successful at it, but you don't have to live in doomsday prep mode. You can't control life, so why would you continue to waste energy trying to control life? Controlling life might be the only thing that is truly impossible.

The most out of control I have ever felt was when I divorced my first wife in 2006. We dated in high school for a couple of years and then reunited in our twenties. We were married for six years, but it was an unhealthy relationship. There were substance abuse issues, and I reached a point where I realized the relationship was never going to be what I wanted. A week after I left the relationship, she made a failed suicide attempt. It was an extremely intense and painful time. I was a mess. This part of my life stretched me in many ways, but that is not relevant to this discussion. I will save it for the next book

For the next year or two, I struggled with my own substance abuse issues, and I started to see a therapist who happened to specialize in aspects of the metaphysical. She taught me how to ground and balance my energy. She taught me how to keep other people's energy out of my energy.

During a session one day, the conversation turned to my fear of the future. I had a feeling that I was destined to serve a higher purpose, but I was scared of taking on that role. I said, "I'm intimidated by the shoes I'm wearing because I know that this path is going to play a role in lifting the consciousness of the planet." It shocked me to hear those words come out of my mouth, and it surprised her too. Something I couldn't comprehend was guiding me toward a future I didn't understand. But, beyond my logical, analytical mind there was a sense of knowing.

That was the beginning of owning my power, owning my abilities. That was the beginning of becoming who I really am—an infinite being. By embracing my gifts, characteristics that once felt like liabilities, the path to finding my role in lifting the consciousness of the planet started to unfold. And now I literally can't stop doing it.

The turmoil that surrounded the end of that relationship had a huge impact on me. It was arguably the worst thing that had ever happened to me, next to the death of my cousin Adam. But without that turmoil, I would not have my current wife, Alexis, and our four boys. If I had not struggled so much at the end of that relationship, I may not have realized the need to explore my full potential. One of the most painfully challenging things in the story of my life enabled the best things in my life. At the time, I wanted to change it, control it, and avoid it. Now I understand that it was a totally necessary part of my journey.

Life takes us through tough, heart-wrenching situations that we want to avoid and control. Sometimes it feels as if we can't trust life. It feels as if we need to try to force life in the direction we want it to go. We worry and manipulate, attempting to protect the things we love and avoid heartbreak and sadness. The truth is, we have no control over the details of our journey, but we can absolutely trust that life is unfolding for our highest and greatest good. Even when it seems impossible to believe that it's true.

Today, I love my life and my family so much, and I wouldn't have them if I had been in complete control back then. The struggle of that divorce turned me into the man I needed to be to have the relationship and career I have now. It was all part of my unique process of life.

I'm going to challenge you with this next concept. *Instead of trying to control the unknown, you need to embrace it.* This paradox may be surprising, uncomfortable even. But if you can rise to this level of awareness, you will save yourself a lot of time, energy, worry, and disappointment.

Achieving the impossible may not happen on your timeline and it almost undoubtedly will not happen exactly as you imagine. The timeline and details are determined by the process of life, which cannot be controlled. Framing a big target as possible doesn't mean you get to set the details and dates. The connections and opportunities that life will bring you to help you do the impossible are unknown. If you put yourself in alignment with who you really are (an infinite being) and what you really want (the impossible), you will hit that target. But life needs the space to move things around and make the impossible possible. Letting the process of life work means finding certainty in the unknown.

Living with certainty in the unknown is letting go of the desire to control the future. How do we get rid of the desire to control the future? We start trusting life. I spent a large portion of my life living in the future. As an achiever, I went to work for a massive, highly influential coaching company so I could figure out how to be my best and control the future. After spending years consumed by my vision of this specific end result, I realized I was missing my present life by avoiding and denying the process of life. I wasn't trusting that life would unfold to maximize my growth and expansion on its timeframe.

Uncertainty—the doubt and fear of the unknown—happens in the present when you're living for the future. When you are focused on a specific vision or expectation of what needs to happen next, you're blocking all other possibilities. You are resisting the present moment. When you resist the present moment, you are not trusting that life is going to unfold in the interest of your highest and greatest self.

CREATING SUCCESS

Success is less about knowing the right actions to take and more about aligning yourself with success and allowing it to happen. Yes, that sounds backward. But it's true.

Here is the conventional formula for success:

RIGHT STRATEGY ➡ **RIGHT ACTION** ➡ **RESULT ACHIEVED**

The formula above is only part of the process. For those who have studied mindset, you may be familiar with this formula:

RIGHT MINDSET ➡ **RIGHT STRATEGY** ➡ **RIGHT ACTION** ➡ **RESULT ACHIEVED**

After working from the elevated mindset formula for years, I realized it was incomplete. The missing piece is *frame*. Here's how success is actually created:

ALIGNED FRAME ➡ **RIGHT MINDSET** ➡ **RIGHT STRATEGY** ➡

RIGHT ACTION ➡ **RESULT ACHIEVED**

WORKING HARD DOES NOT CREATE SUCCESS

Have you ever put in hard work and not gotten the results? Maybe you have put in years of hard work, and success consistently evaded you. You aren't getting the results because you are out of alignment with the target.

Sometimes hard work *can* be the catalyst for getting into alignment with success. As a result, we are socially conditioned to believe that hard work creates success. It doesn't. Alignment with success creates success. More accurately, alignment with success makes success your state of being.

It's true that the more you work, the more opportunities for alignment you have. But why would you want to work yourself into alignment when you can simply start from an aligned frame? The process hinges on starting from a place of alignment in order to eliminate hard work and take the glory out of grinding.

Our current culture glorifies grinding. We have been programmed to forget that grinding is pushing against resistance. Resistance is an indication of misalignment. Do you really want to spend your life grinding? Or would you like to create success with ease and flow? Look at the super-successful entrepreneur Gary Vaynerchuk, for example. (If you don't know of him, look him up. He is amazing.) Gary is a big proponent of grinding—he calls it "hustling."

Having never met Gary, I can't be sure, but when I look at him, I don't see someone who is simply working hard and hustling. I see a highly motivated infinite being working from an aligned frame embracing the unknown on his unique path. Gary Vaynerchuk is in flow. Taking action, closing deals, creating tons of content, and constantly connecting with the unbounded possibilities of the unknown, Gary is doing *his* thing. Though it may look and sound like hustling to most of us, Gary is not grinding against resistance. He is trusting the process of life while staying in action.

Framing is the formula for getting everything you want. Yes, a large volume of work will be necessary. But *hard* work is not a requirement. Alignment is the main requirement. Now that you have access to framing, you also have a choice. You can spend countless hours working "hard" and possibly end up in alignment with your target. Or, by starting in an aligned frame, you can radically shorten the process and reduce the amount of trial and error required to hit a target. Instead of years spent practicing and failing, you can cut the process down to months.

When you start in a frame where success is your state of being, your mindset is aligned with success. Mindset alignment with your target creates naturally inspired strategy. A naturally inspired strategy leads you to the right action, which hits the target.

Think of a time when you were extremely focused and committed to a target. Yet no matter what you did you could not close the deal. You wanted things to move in a certain direction, but they wouldn't budge. You put in hours and hours of hard work but couldn't make it happen. Despite all your effort, hard work did not create success.

If hard work created success, we'd all be billionaires.

Believing hard work is the main requirement for achieving success seems logical. How many times have you told yourself, *If I want to be successful, I have to work hard*? Again, it all comes back to our beliefs.

Remember, for every belief, the inverse is true. If you believe *I have to work hard to be successful,* by default you believe that *If I don't work hard, I won't be successful.* Your rules (your beliefs) for becoming successful may be exactly what is keeping you from being successful!

From an elevated perspective, success is not an achievement but a state of being. Success breeds success. Lack of success breeds lack of success. Conventionally, success is something you create through volume of work, but that does not have to be your reality. Success can begin the moment you set your frame with success as your state of being. *You can either start in success or you can spend endless hours grinding, trying to get success.* For me, the choice is clear.

In coaching, I often see clients struggle because they are working from a lack of success. By believing they have to *do* something in order to become successful, they are creating resistance to their end target. In that environment of operation (frame), taking action is the only key to creating success.

The reality is that success comes from alignment with success, not action. You must take action—often a lot of action—to close deals, make connections, and pursue your passion. But volume and intensity of work are not required components of success. You are either in a frame that is aligned with success or in a frame misaligned with success. No amount of action taken in misalignment will produce a state of success.

Alignment creates success. Not hard work.

CHECKING FOR ALIGNMENT

At this point, you know that as an infinite being living in an attraction-based universe, starting from a frame of success will attract success. You understand that starting in alignment with success creates accelerated growth and expansion. The next logical question is, *How do I know if I am in alignment?* Simple. You can actually feel it. Your emotions are your guide.

Ask yourself:

- *Do I feel flow on my path? Or do I feel resistance?*
- *Am I taking naturally inspired action? Or am I grinding and forcing myself to take action?*

Emotions are your built-in guidance system. The problem is that most of us have been trained not to trust, or even acknowledge, this invaluable resource. Past experiences and social conditioning often cause us to question and dismiss our instinct. To check alignment, get in touch with your instinct. I like to call it your *knowing*. If you follow the process (and believe it will work), you will become more connected with your knowing and will instantly, easily identify alignment and misalignment by how you feel.

SEVEN LEVELS OF MINDSET ALIGNMENT

After I discovered framing, my capacity for further tuning my frequency expanded and revealed the different levels of alignment. The highest level is *active creation*, which signifies following your knowing to take naturally inspired action with ease and flow. The lowest level—*in reaction to the past*—indicates a past experience is limiting future success and possibility. Evaluating your level of mindset alignment in relation to a specific area of your life highlights potential for improvement and allows you to focus your awareness appropriately and strategically.

LEVEL 7   Active creation

LEVEL 6   Aligned with future wants and desires

LEVEL 5   Open with positive expectation

LEVEL 4   Open neutral

LEVEL 3   Open with doubt

LEVEL 2   Limited by the past
(re-creating past limitations)

LEVEL 1   In reaction to the past

When evaluating mindset, the level of alignment is relative to the subject. For example, while your relationship mindset may currently be a three, your business mindset level could be a five. Your mindset alignment level depends on where you are in that specific area of your life.

1. *In reaction to the past*—Unable to function or grow. Stuck in reaction to the past. Many times, this can be trauma related.
2. *Limited by the past (re-creating past limitations)*—Doesn't realize the next moment is full of possibility. Repeating behaviors and actions based on past experiences.

3. *Open with doubt*—Believes anything is possible but doubts what happens next will be positive. Stuck in resistance.
4. *Open neutral*—Completely open. Believes anything can happen but has no stance on whether it will be positive or negative.
5. *Open with positive expectation*—Believes anything is possible and what happens next will most likely be positive. Holding on to some resistance.
6. *Aligned with future wants and desires*—Positive alignment with inspired action. Feels positive about actions taken. Aligned with targets and purpose. No resistance.
7. *Active creation*—Aligned with what is happening in the future. Working with life to create and shape the future. Beyond resistance.

When I discovered the seven levels of mindset alignment, things started to change, though not immediately. Initially, I didn't completely understand *active creation*. More had to be revealed before I could describe and teach it. I had to go through the process of life and align myself with the future me who understood how to share this empowering tool. Today, I can teach active creation, and that's what I hope you learn from this book—how to work with life to create and shape a future by finding certainty in the unknown.

Let's get into alignment. Answer these questions:
- Are you starting to understand that alignment is what creates success, not hard work?
- Are you starting to understand the ways to get into alignment with what you want?
- Are you ready to learn even more powerful ways to get into alignment with what you want?

Now let's integrate.

Repeat After Me (out loud):

- I take full ownership of my life and everything in it.
- I take full ownership of my past, present, and future.
- I understand that alignment with success creates success, not hard work.
- I understand that in order to do the impossible, I have to get comfortable operating in the unknown. Because that's where the magic happens. .
- I understand that in the next moment anything can happen. So from this moment on, I hereby choose to operate in a frame where new ideas, new connections, and new opportunities easily find me.
- I understand that any action I take out of alignment is pointless because I will never hit the target unless I'm in alignment with it.
- So I choose to always start in alignment.
- I command my subconscious mind to automatically bring to my attention when I am operating out of alignment.
- I choose to live in a reality where I notice when I am out of alignment with my target.
- I choose to live in a reality where getting into alignment with my target is a natural, easy thing to do.
- From this moment on, I understand that I can create any success I want by simply getting into alignment with it.
- I understand that doing the impossible does require work, but hard work is not what creates success; alignment does.
- I understand that there are seven levels of mindset alignment.
- I choose to believe this 100 percent, past, present, and future—all versions of me. And I immediately take ownership of anything contradictory to this and integrate all of it now.

Frame-Shifting Exercise

- Can you get a sense of a future version of you that starts all action in alignment?
- Can you imagine a version of you in the future that is very clear and aware of when you are out of alignment?
- Can you get a sense of a future version of you who understands these concepts so well that you can teach them to other people?
- Can you get a sense of a future version of you that loves shifting your mindset because you know it's how you create your own reality?

Great. Hold your awareness on that version of you for ten seconds. How do you feel now?

Chapter Seven
PICKING THE RIGHT TARGET

Life does not reward mediocrity. To win big, you have to play at the level you are destined to play.

Our purpose in life is to grow, evolve, and expand. With that in mind, should you pick targets that encourage growth or targets that maintain your current level of success? The answer is obvious. We should all be picking targets that initiate, encourage, and require tapping into your full potential.

FOLLOW YOUR KNOWING
When you swing for the fence or play outside the box, it may be unsettling to people around you and cause them to reject big targets as illogical and irresponsible. As I mentioned before, I have experienced this in my life. Trusting your passion

and following your knowing can be difficult when the people around you are questioning your decision to go big.

During my first six years of coaching, I was basically broke. At one point my family was on state food assistance. After I left my career in tech sales to follow my passion for coaching, there was friction at home. Coming from a place of love (and fear), my family was concerned about my decision.

As much as it hurt to hear that perspective, I knew if I stopped pursuing my coaching career, it would crush me and haunt me for the rest of my life. I had found my passion; I couldn't stop. My internal drive and desire to become a coach was too intense to ignore. I had to go big. Struggle and conflict were imperative to uncovering the specific lessons life had in store for me. Learning to trust and follow my knowing, despite the discomfort of receiving pushback from those I love, was one of those crucial lessons.

The only person who can honestly know you is you. How could anyone else know you better than yourself? No one knows what it's like to be in your body, to feel what you feel, or to think what you think. Therefore, any negative input you receive from other people concerning your goals, your targets, or your passion is simply one infinite being judging another infinite being for stepping outside of their comfort zone.

The bottom line is: You *must play at the level you are meant to play*. Exploring our full potential allows life to bring us the lessons, resources, and connections needed to find and follow our passion. There is nothing more exciting than expanding to become the person you know you were meant to be.

Ask yourself these questions:

- Am I currently playing at the level I should be?
- Am I growing and expanding by building on my previous successes? Or am I limiting my potential by focusing on past failures?
- Is there a past failure that was so painful I have decided never to go big again?
- Have I experienced rejection from peers and loved ones for thinking about or going "too big"?

THE PROBLEM WITH SMALL TARGETS

Settling for average results and repeating tried-and-true patterns is logical and responsible, but what is the real reason most people aren't doing the impossible? The main reason for sticking to small targets is the emotional reaction to big targets. Underlying or explicit fear around big targets often drives us to keep aiming low.

Small targets are safe and reliable because we already know how to hit the mark. The problem with small targets is they lack inspiration. There is nothing exciting about being average or maintaining the same level of income with incremental annual growth.

When I started chasing big targets, I felt more alive than ever before. I felt pulled, compelled, and ignited. Filled with new ideas, motivation, and inspiration, I knew I was following my knowing, instead of just my thinking, because I could feel it.

Let's say you made $100,000 last year. If you set your goals for the coming years and aim for $105,000 or $110,000, you probably already know what to do to accomplish that level of growth. When we base goals on (small) incremental growth, the typical approach is to repeat past strategies with reasonable expansion. Staying in the world of incremental growth seems comfortable, which is fine. But if you want to access your full potential, you have to start aiming higher and embracing growth.

Why wouldn't you aim to make $500,000 or $1 million when all that is required is growth? Why would you keep aiming at the target you've already hit because you think it's comfortable? Struggling to get by in life with limited financial resources, working ridiculous hours, and not ever experiencing the success you desire isn't comfortable. The truth is there is nothing more painful than being average. You were not born to be average. You are destined to be exceptional. Again, you may be wired to seek comfort, but you were born for greatness.

Moving beyond your comfort zone is challenging, but it is also exhilarating. Aiming for a bigger target stretches you beyond your current capacity into your next major growth area. The growth required can be daunting, but the buildup—the fear and the doubt before the action—is actually worse than the experience. If you are avoiding growth and expansion, you are missing the excitement of pursuing greatness. To begin, align your frame with expansion and growth. When that is your starting point, moving through new lessons and experiences becomes easier and less intimidating.

Obviously, playing life at a lower level produces smaller results. If you want to play at a higher level, you must aim higher. Remember, in the next moment anything can happen, especially in business. One phone call can be a complete game changer. Shifting your mindset to embrace this truth sets you free from basing your future success on results of the past.

My greatest wish for you is that you decide to go big and follow your knowing to find the work you are destined to do. May the process help reveal your true path and the work you cannot *not* do. Because that work—your mission—changes the world.

WHAT IS AN IMPOSSIBLE TARGET?

Conditioned to follow arbitrary rules, we label something impossible and make it so. But a big, seemingly impossible, target is just like any other target. Big targets are not impossible; they are simply uncommon because they are unconventional. If you grew up in an environment where pursuing impossible targets was the norm, you would naturally do the same. Aligning frame with possibility, as opposed to impossibility, gives you ownership of your environment and removes socially conditioned resistance. Alignment, strategy, and action are the way to hit any target, no matter how ambitious.

Different targets trigger different emotions. We often consider a target impossible because we are disempowered by feelings of fear and doubt. To move beyond reaction and into active creation, we need to shift our frame around selecting targets. Proper perspective allows us to face the fear and doubt that too often convinces us to settle for mediocrity and blocks us from greatness.

Negative emotions arise around aiming higher because going big pushes us out of our comfort zone and into a growth zone. Shooting for a higher target is about choosing growth over comfort. An impossible target can become attainable, and enjoyable, when we shift to a higher frequency that is aligned with expanding capability with ease and flow.

When an infinite being, a bundle of pure energy, switches to a higher frequency, the shift is felt in the body. We feel uncertainty, fear, and expansion, all of which are merely the side effects of transformational growth. We should welcome these side effects and make note of them as they are the indicators of our pathway.

Any negative emotion you feel about a target is simply the misalignment between your present frame and the mindset you need to hit the mark. Fear and doubt are not telling you to turn back. They are telling you it's time to meet the moment with growth. Don't be afraid of the feelings that accompany growth. Once you start taking action, those feelings will go away.

Our emotions, both positive and negative, are indicators that life has something to show us. Life is saying, "I need your attention here. I need you fully present for this one because it is going to change you in the most amazing way."

THE DIFFERENCE BETWEEN BIG AND SMALL TARGETS

Swinging the bat slower doesn't make it easier to get a hit.

The only difference between big and small targets is strategy. Imagine you are the captain of a ship at sea. As the captain, you have the power to pick your destination. Once you pick the destination, your job is to align the ship with the correct course and do the work needed to complete that journey. This will be true no matter which destination you select. Your strategy to reach each possible destination will be different. Yet every destination will require action and alignment to complete the trip. Ultimately, your results will be determined by the direction you point your ship, not by the type of work or the amount of time spent at sea.

Financial targets may seem more complicated, but they are just as simple. You could point your ship in one direction and aim to make $100,000. Or you could point your ship in other directions and aim to make $500,000 or $1 million. Alignment and action are the key to hitting any target. The size of the target is completely irrelevant. You can point your ship in any direction you want. It is the direction in which you aim that determines your results.

Hitting a big target or a small target is the exact same process but with a different strategy. Remember how success is created:

ALIGNED FRAME → **RIGHT MINDSET** → **RIGHT STRATEGY** →
RIGHT ACTION → **RESULT ACHIEVED**

When we pick a target that requires expanding our knowledge and capability, we start playing life at higher level. No matter your age, passion, or career path, life will reward you when you rise to the challenge of aiming higher. You will gain new insights, new ideas, and new inspirations. Resources will show up, and connections will be made. Life is designed to support you through accelerated growth.

Timeframes for hitting specific targets are contingent on the process of life, but that doesn't mean we shouldn't go big. It took years to start my coaching company because the process of life needed time to prepare me for that reality. I have also expanded my business by 10 times in one quarter. Both were exciting, transformational experiences that started with deciding to go big. Believing radically accelerated growth is possible makes me less concerned with how long it will take me to hit the mark and more focused on aligning myself with big targets.

If your frequency is in alignment with your target, it will happen. That's how life works. It has nothing to do with worthiness or earning it. It's mathematical.

Once you understand how life really works (which we will discuss further in the next chapter), aiming for greatness by picking the right target becomes the easy part. What can be challenging is getting into alignment with an impossible target.

Meeting this obstacle requires showing up as the real you. Allow the process of life to push and stretch you into who you're supposed to become. If you are willing to follow your expansion, be honest with yourself through humility and openness, and face your next growth area, you can absolutely hit impossible targets over and over again.

"Going big" doesn't mean taking big risks. It means reframing what is possible by pushing past emotional discomfort. The sooner you go big, the sooner you will have amazing results. You will not avoid fear and pain by playing small, you will actually spend more time in both.

PICKING THE RIGHT TARGET

Picking the right target is paramount. It's the difference between struggle and flow. It's the difference between settling for average and elevated success. It's the difference between unremarkable mediocrity and the world of the outstanding.

The right target propels and inspires action. The right target creates passion, motivation, and excitement. When you pick the right target, it's like being hit by lightning. That's how I felt when my first coach, Michael Savage, asked me, "Have you ever thought of becoming a coach?"

It felt like a power surge. The hair on the back of my neck stood up, my heart raced, and I even got a little sweat on my brow. For the first time, I was excited about learning. It was exhilarating. I was just as motivated by the journey as I was about the end result, and I couldn't stop thinking about it. Consumed by the energy of this possibility, I knew I had found my passion.

Of course, not every target has that impact, but it is important to have at least one target you are passionate about. Think about it for second. Can you enjoy your life more by following and chasing and going after something that excites you and inspires you? Or by being comfortable doing what's easy? When have you felt most alive in your life? Was it when you were taking on difficult things or easy things?

As infinite beings, the potential for greatness resides in all of us. The path toward doing the work you were born to do is your future—if you choose it. If you are currently seeking success solely to make money so you can retire, I believe it is because you have yet to find your passion. If your goal is to stop working, you simply haven't found your mission.

It's not bad to want to make money so you can retire, and there are many great books out there on the topic—like *Set for Life* by Scott Trench or *The 4-Hour Work Week* by Tim Ferriss. That's how I started: I thought my path was to become financially independent so I could avoid the work I didn't like. Then, the process of life revealed my mission, and my life transformed.

QUESTIONS TO HELP YOU PICK THE RIGHT TARGET (REVIEW)

Here are three questions to help get clarity on picking the right target. You can use these questions repeatedly throughout your journey. These are the exact questions I ask when I coach clients to help uncover passion and reveal inspiration:

1. What do I want?
2. What is possible?
3. What is impossible but would be fun to do anyway?

The first question—*What do I want?*—is where most people spend the majority of their time. The problem with this question is the answer is likely to be based on past references. The target produced is likely to match your current level of success.

The second question—*What is possible?*—is a better question than the first because it is based on an external reference or what we've seen other people do. That is, unless you're beyond external reference because you're already living in the land of greatness.

The third question—*What is impossible but would be fun to do anyway?*—is based on your internal reference or your knowing. Ask this question and watch the magic show up.

Your internal world is where inspiration happens. This is the land of flow and naturally inspired action. This is where you want to live. Operating from your passion with flow is the best feeling you can have in life.

If failing was impossible, success was guaranteed, and you could do anything, what would you do?

LET'S DO THE IMPOSSIBLE

Do the Impossible Principles (Ideas)

1. You are unlimited.

2. Anything can happen next.

3. The past doesn't matter.

4. The only prerequisite for success is alignment with it.

5. You are complete; there is nothing wrong with you.

6. The present is the result of the past, not an indicator of the future.

7. You are one moment away from a new idea, connection, or opportunity that will radically transform your world.

Do the Impossible Rules (Actions)

1. You've got to aim much, much higher.

2. Pick the right starting point.

3. Never start in reaction.

4. Rushing slows the process (savoring the process accelerates it).

5. If you know exactly what to do, you're not aiming high enough.

Let's get into alignment. Answer these questions:

- Are you ready to aim higher than ever before?
- Are you ready to hit big targets?
- Are you ready to pick targets that inspire you even when you don't know how to hit them?

Now let's integrate.

Repeat After Me (out loud):

- *I take full ownership of my life and everything in it.*
- *I take full ownership of my past, present, and future.*
- *I understand that to get the best possible result, I need to aim at the best possible target.*
- *I understand that most people aim way too low because anything is possible in the next moment.*
- *I understand that if I know how to hit my target, I'm not aiming high enough.*
- *I allow myself to go big.*
- *I allow myself to go really, really big.*
- *I choose to easily identify uncommon, impossible targets that excite me.*
- *I choose to live in a reality of naturally inspired action, which comes from aiming at the most amazing targets I can think of, even when I don't know how to hit them.*
- *I'm ready to do the impossible.*
- *I am doing the impossible.*
- *I understand the Do the Impossible principles.*
- *I understand the Do the Impossible rules.*
- *I'm ready to aim much, much higher.*
- *I choose to believe this 100 percent, past, present, and future—all versions of me. And I immediately take ownership of anything contradictory to this and integrate all of it now.*

Frame-Shifting Exercise

- Can you get a sense of a future version of you that feels inspired and excited about your goals?
- Can you imagine a version of you in the future that knows how to pick the right target?
- Can you get a sense of a future version of you that has hit an impossible target and is already working on the next impossible target?
- Can you get a sense of a future version of you that has hit so many impossible targets that you inspire people around you to do the same?

Great. Hold your awareness on that version of you for ten seconds. How do you feel now?

Chapter Eight

HOW LIFE REALLY WORKS

You will get that which you are a frequency match to.

Discovering how life really works has been the biggest game changer in creating the reality I want to experience and feeling the way I want to feel. It impacts all areas of my life, not just business and performance. Knowing the truth about how life works continues to strengthen my belief in the process. As my belief grows, my ability to reshape my reality expands.

Grasping these concepts can create a monumental shift in your life. It changed everything for me and many of my coaching clients. Getting to this point of understanding took me two decades. But those years of searching for the process were required so that others could create success more quickly and with more ease, without spending unnecessary time in trial and error.

Most people spend their time focused on the wrong component of success.

Believing the most important element is volume of action, they concentrate on strategizing and working hard. The problem is that they are often in misalignment with success because they are in the wrong frame. No amount of action taken out of alignment will get the desired result. The key to how life works is aligning your frame with your target.

This is the conventional success formula:

CREATE A PLAN ➡️ **TAKE ACTION** ➡️ **GET THE RESULT**

Correct, but incomplete, this formula is the way most people believe life works. There are countless ways to approach these three steps. Many coaches, podcasts, systems, tools, and methodologies use and discuss this formula to create success. Unfortunately, this is only part of the equation. And more importantly, it's the least important part.

For years, I followed this pattern. I was a grinder and sought to push through all forms of resistance as I mimicked the habits and behaviors of successful people. I even adopted practices like taking cold showers and shouting myself into elevated states. Despite doing everything I could think of to hit my target, it didn't work. After discovering framing, I realized I was missing the most crucial pieces of the equation: frame and the process of life.

This is the success formula of the process (how life really works):

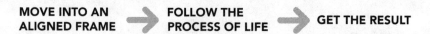

MOVE INTO AN ALIGNED FRAME ➡️ **FOLLOW THE PROCESS OF LIFE** ➡️ **GET THE RESULT**

Your frame determines the frequency of your energy. Life responds to you based on that frequency. As an infinite being operating in an attraction-based universe, you are not a victim to life. You are actively creating every part of your reality based on your frame. If you don't like what you're experiencing, you are in the wrong frame.

Here's a simple way to think about it: Imagine life is like playing a video game in which you are the player *and* the creator. If you don't like the game, you have the ability to design a new one.

Reshaping your reality can give you access to more joy, more time, more freedom, and more money, and all with ease and flow. But you have to believe it works. And you have to take the action your aligned frame inspires.

THE ACCIDENTAL EXPERIMENT THAT CHANGED MY LIFE

It may surprise you to know that a major catalyst for my discovering the process involved quitting. Following the conventional success formula had led me to a dead end, and I simply gave up. Facing failure, at one of the lowest moments of my career, I quit. For years, I tried to force success, but it wasn't until I stopped trying to control life that I began to see results I didn't even know were possible.

After starting a series of failed companies, I founded a business coaching company called Excel Coaching with two partners. Instead of putting my name on the company, we named it Excel because I wasn't ready to be visible. Unconsciously, I wanted to hide. Part of me still didn't think I was good enough.

Obsessed with starting a successful coaching company, I thought this was *it*. My partners and I worked hard every day trying to land clients. But after five months of grinding, we had not gained a single client. It was unbelievable.

Having spent years in coaching, both as a client and a coach, I believed that if you followed your passion and worked hard, you would be successful. The failure of Excel shattered everything I thought I knew about life. I literally gave up. At the time, I thought I was quitting. Now I know it was actually a surrender.

Wondering if I was even supposed to be a coach, I didn't know what to do other than wave a white flag at life. While I was considering going back to technology sales, something shifted. And magic started to happen.

Out of nowhere, I picked up three coaching contracts. All three were referral clients who came to me without pursuit. It was a shock. The company I dreamed of starting began to gain momentum and flourish. Today it is known as Jason Drees Coaching.

This was the accidental experiment that changed my life. Yes, it was painful and scary, but on the other side of the pain and fear was the expansion and growth I had been seeking. Before that moment and with the best intentions, I was neck deep in a misguided attempt at controlling life. My breakthrough required getting beat down enough to surrender to the process of life. Once I released my imagined control, my world opened to endless possibilities.

Today I get into alignment with life instead of trying to control it. I let the process determine my path and don't try to force things in a certain direction.

It was a very frustrating experience, and I bet you can relate. Constantly striving but never getting what you want is exhausting. Time and again, I would pick a target and take action, but I couldn't get the result.

What do you do when you don't get your desired result? Do you work harder? Do you copy other people's patterns for achieving success? Do you start beating yourself up? Can you relate to relying on those tired tactics? If you are working harder, trying new strategies, and still aren't getting results, you are in a misaligned mindset and a disempowered frame. I know because I was there. I still find myself there sometimes.

Even though I know how life works, I still experience the fear and doubt that comes from not trusting the process of life. It is a part of my constant growth and expansion. The difference now is that when those negative feelings arise, I know the truth. Recognizing fear and doubt as indicators of opportunity for growth, I check my frame as opposed to just working harder.

When life isn't working the way we believe it should, we often:

work harder

copy other people's patterns

work even harder

beat ourselves up

This creates:

more resistance

more misalignment

stronger negative beliefs around
a specific subject or action

a disempowered frame

SHIFTING FROM REACTION TO CREATION

When I founded Excel Coaching, I started from a place of reaction to my past and my current life situation. Being afraid to put my name on the business was an indicator that I was not aligned with success. Negative identity beliefs kept me in reaction to the past and blocked me from embracing what was possible in the future. At that time, I wasn't ready to take full ownership of my destiny. Therefore, I couldn't be the active creator of my life, and as a result, the company failed.

Once I recognized this trait in myself, I found that many people are spending their life in reaction to the past. When you make the shift from living in reaction to living in creation, a world of possibility opens. There are a few concepts that can help make that subtle, but vital, shift easier.

Everything in your life right now is what it is. In this moment, your bank account reflects your past decisions. Your career is the combination of all the jobs you've ever had. The quality of your relationships is the direct result of how you have treated people in the past. In this moment, you cannot change your bank account, career, or relationships. Your life circumstances are in a fixed position in the present.

The state of everything in your life in the present moment is a result of the past. Before you move into regret, I have empowering news. The present is a result of your past, but the present is not an indicator of the future. And the future is where you have the ability to harness the power of mindset.

A common challenge I see my clients encounter is trying to shape the future while starting in reaction to the past. Though it is perfectly normal, it is not the best way to operate.

When your starting point is rooted in reaction to the past, you are starting in a hole. Like sailing into a headwind, you are starting in resistance. You want to start with momentum. You want to start with the wind at your back. You want to start in success.

Success isn't something you create. Success is something you *are*. If you believe you have to work hard to *become* successful, you have already made your journey longer and more strenuous before it has even begun. Living in active creation involves seeing and embracing success as a state of being. When success is your state of being, you will attract it because at the frame level, you are a frequency match to success.

THE FORMULA FOR HOW LIFE WORKS

Now that you've made it further,
here is the complete formula for how life works:

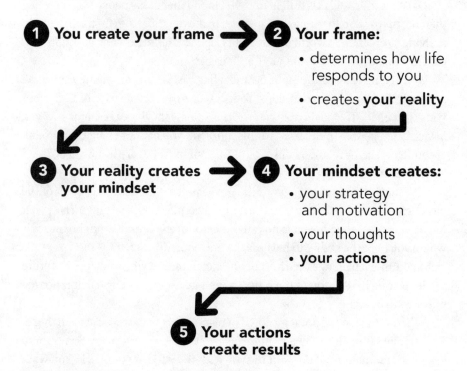

1 **You create your frame** ➡ **2** **Your frame:**

- determines how life responds to you
- creates **your reality**

3 **Your reality creates your mindset** ➡ **4** **Your mindset creates:**

- your strategy and motivation
- your thoughts
- **your actions**

5 **Your actions create results**

YOU CAN'T SKIP THE PROCESS

Life is a process. There are no shortcuts. If you want to climb a mountain, you can't make it to the top by skipping a section. If you rush through a section you want to avoid, you may fall, undoing some of the progress you made.

Your life process is unique to your life experience. By trying to rush through an experience, you are denying the value of that moment and the lessons life is bringing you. Rushing slows down the process of life because it is evidence that you are trying to skip the present moment.

Trusting the process of life while accepting its timeframe is the quickest way to the end result. When we are on vacation, time often seems to fly by. Why is that? Because on vacation we are concentrated on savoring the moment as opposed to rushing through it. The way to accelerate the process is by savoring each section and appreciating the process for what it is—your unique journey.

Chapter Nine

THE FRAME-SHIFTING PROCESS

As I've been mastering the process over the past year, I've experienced deals pop up out of nowhere. I've had innovative ideas for Jason Drees Coaching, including services that have initiated radical growth in just a few weeks and opportunities that have the potential to generate a seven-figure revenue stream within a year. I've had new people come into my life and join my team at exactly the right moment. All simply by shifting my frame.

Honestly, sometimes I still can't believe it is this easy. I continue to be amazed at the life-changing power of this technique. As I teach more and more people the process, I'm witnessing more and more people have the same experience.

WHAT IS A FRAME?

Your frame is your consciousness or the awareness that is you. It is you as a being. It is all of you. Your frame interacts with life and directs how life responds to you. Your frame establishes your vibrational frequency.

You control your frame, usually unconsciously. Your frame decides if you have a good day or a bad day. It determines whether you continue operating at the same level or whether you expand into doing the impossible.

Before we get too far into frame, let's review. You are an infinite being made of atoms and pure energy, living in an attraction-based universe made almost entirely of energy. The reality you experience is based on your frequency. Life responds to the vibrational energy produced by your frame. Basically, in every moment, you are broadcasting a signal, informing life who you are, what you want, and what you expect. Your frame creates that signal.

Considering all of this, doesn't it make sense that the vibrational universe responds to you as a vibrational being?

HOW IS YOUR FRAME CREATED?

Just as you are always in a mindset, you are always in a frame. The distinction between mindset and frame is level of awareness. Frame shifting involves holding the awareness of a future version of yourself, which shifts your mindset (your operating system) to a higher level of capacity and capability.

Frame determines your expectations (mindset and beliefs). You have expectations for almost everything, including how life works, how people act, the weather, how your day will go, if you will close a deal, if a new hire will work out, and everything else you encounter. And all of those expectations are constantly influencing and dictating your reality. At the action or subject level, your expectations inform your day-to-day experience of life. But the expectations originate beyond your beliefs and above your mindset in your frame.

Taking ownership of your expectations can seem complicated. One endlessly empowering aspect of framing is it removes the complication of analyzing current expectations by moving directly to creating aligned expectations. Focusing your awareness on what you want and who you want to be activates attraction without obsessing over the details at the action level.

Are you starting to understand? Are you starting to see yourself as the creator of your reality? Are you beginning to believe that while playing the video game of life you are also creating it?

It can be a lot to handle, but it's true. If you're having trouble believing this, I suggest continuing to explore it as an idea. That's where I started. It all began as an experiment around a new concept. As it was validated over and over again, I gathered so much proof that I could no longer doubt the power of framing. Most recently, I've tested it in group coaching and witnessed both new and established clients experience accelerated transformation and success.

If you believe what I'm presenting, it means you are in a frame that believes it. If you have disbelief, you are in a frame of disbelief. Moving into a frame of belief is as simple as holding the awareness of a future version of you that believes frame shifting works. Can you access that awareness? Can you imagine that version of you and how it feels to believe in framing?

Much like mindset, your frame is created by your past. Your frame is created by your experience of life and your life experience. This means that the way you view the world is influenced by both your day-to-day feelings and emotions (experience of life) and the way you view the story of your life as a whole (life experience). I'm sure it is no surprise that social conditioning is another factor that impacts your frame. Your brain is constantly analyzing all you encounter and creating expectations and understandings about how life works. As discussed previously, these are your beliefs, which are components of your frame. Frame is at the macro level. Beliefs are at the micro level.

What you've been conditioned to believe about creating success may be the very thing that is blocking you from achieving it. When you use a conventional approach, your beliefs need to be changed first to shift your mindset and switch your frame. When we flip that concept, by first taking ownership of our reality, we can change our beliefs from the top down, starting with frame.

IT'S ALL FRAMES

We all want more time, more money (resources), and more freedom, which depend on new and different connections and interactions with people. What determines the type of people we meet? What determines the success of a new business? I could never answer these questions before. Now I can. It all hinges on framing.

At any moment, you are operating within many frames. You have frames about work, frames about relationships, frames about food, and frames about money. You even have frames about driving on the freeway and how other people should drive. Every area of your life has its own frame.

The way to shape your reality is by consciously shifting the frame relative to what you want. If you want to make more money, you need to shift your frame around money.

The first step is to stop reacting to your current reality. Again, your current life situation cannot be altered. Everything in your life right now is a result of everything you've done prior to now. A higher understanding of this is that everything in your life right now is the result of who you have been (your frequency) and what you have attracted.

The present moment is not an indicator of the future; it is the result of the past. This is where a lot of people get stuck, constantly reacting to the present and letting it dictate their future. Reacting to the present is pointless because you already attracted and created it. Embrace your past and present as important experiences and move into creating your future by becoming what you want so you will attract what you want.

Frame shifting is the process of selecting your version of reality. This simple understanding has been crucial to expanding my ability to deal with things I find undesirable. When I have a negative emotional reaction to the present moment, I know it is a result of the past. Through practice, I've become effective at letting go of unwanted emotions. If I don't like my present reality, I focus my awareness on creating a new reality.

When you leave the world of reaction and move into the world of creation, *everything* changes. Your negative reactions start to reduce or even disappear. You begin to see all reactions as guides, telling you it is time to shift into a better version of yourself. Reactions become welcome indicators that you have access to a higher frame. We can let our reactions control us, which is basically like having a tantrum and screaming, "I don't like what I created!" Or we can take control and shift frames.

It's all frames.

HOW TO SHIFT FRAMES

Your frame determines the version of life you experience. Frame shifting is how you reshape your reality. While it may seem complicated, frame shifting is actually simple once you understand the concept

The previous sections of this book were designed to give you a new environment of operation where you can easily and consciously shift the frame. Have you begun to view things differently yet? Are you starting to think differently now too? You probably are because I've been shifting your frame since page one. My gift in this life is shifting other people's frames.

Frame shifting is about awareness not visualization. Do not visualize. Seek an awareness. Visualizing uses your brain and will produce your current physical fixed frame. When you get a sense of the future version of you, it is an awareness beyond your physical being. Have you ever been sitting at a stoplight, and you know the person in the car next to you is looking at you? You can't see them, but you can feel their attention on you. That is awareness.

Let's shift frames right now

- Can you get a sense of a version of you, from any time in the future, that completely understands these concepts?
- Can you get a sense of a future version of you that not only understands the process but can teach it?
- Can you get a sense of a future version of you that has been implementing frame shifting for six months and has seen amazing results?
- Can you get a sense of a future version of you that has mastered frame shifting for five years?

Hold your awareness on that version of you for ten seconds.

How do you feel now? Lighter? More certain? Clearer? If the answer to any of those questions is yes, you just shifted frames. It's really that simple. You are now that version of you who can become anything you want. You really are that powerful, if you believe you are.

You have been unconsciously shifting frames your whole life. Right now, you are the most you have ever been. As you gain information and experience, your frame shifts, meaning every day your energy expands, putting you at an increasingly higher vibration. As you grow and learn, your frames shift.

Sometimes frames from the past resurface, triggering negative emotions. Have you ever had a memory pop up that revives the feelings associated with a past experience? You feel the negative emotions from the experience as if it had just happened. In that moment, you shifted to an old frame and a lower vibrational frequency. That's why it feels bad. Moving into a frame (energy/frequency) that is lower than your current level never feels good.

Moving into a future frame always feels good. It usually shows up as feeling lighter and more certain. Just like we when we frame shifted a few moments ago.

You can become an old version or a new version of yourself within a moment. You can't control life, but you can reshape your reality by selecting the version of you that shows up to meet life. Now, do you accept how powerful you are? If so, you are ready to do the impossible.

Instead of spending time in reaction to your present life, shift to the future version of you who knows exactly how to conquer what's next.

HOW FRAME SHIFTING WORKS

Frame shifting is the process of focusing your awareness (which focuses the energy of you) on what you want and aligns your mindset. By holding your awareness for ten seconds on the frame you want, you automatically match the frequency of that frame. The simplest way to do this is to focus on a future version of you who has the thing you want. This could be an idea, it could be a physical result, or it could be simply knowing what to do at work today.

I'm using this exact technique to write this book. As I write, new content is being created because I'm simply starting in a frame where new content is created during the writing process. Additionally, writing this book is transforming me because I also started in a frame where writing this book *is* going to transform me.

Become the person who has what you want, and then what you want will show up. If you misplace your keys and you run around the house saying, "I can't find my keys. I can't find my keys." You will never find your keys. If you walk around the house saying, "I know where my keys are. I know where my keys are." You will find them. If you lose a train of thought, say to yourself, *I know it'll come back in a second*. And it will.

The more you use the process of frame shifting, the faster and easier it becomes. When I started writing this chapter, I was struggling with how to describe framing in a simple, straightforward way. So I asked myself: *Can you get a sense of the future version of you that has just written an amazing chapter on the framing process?* I held the awareness for ten seconds, and the thoughts started flowing. In fact, that is how I've written most of this book. Knowing how to create an idea is active creation (the highest level of mindset alignment) at work. It's also a very cool experience.

HOW LONG DOES IT TAKE TO SHIFT YOUR FRAME?

Frame shifting happens in moments. In my experience, it takes about ten seconds to shift to a new frame. However, during my frame-shifting practice, I've noticed a few things that can delay the process.

One reason for a delay is another frame exists above the frame I am seeking. For example, when I was writing a previous chapter I was stuck. Frame shifting was not working. When I reviewed my frame, I noticed that I was operating in a larger frame of uncertainty, meaning I was not operating in a frame that was 100 percent certain I could write an empowering chapter. My global frame was only 80 percent certain. Therefore, I wasn't able to align with the content because my global frame was out of alignment.

Other things can also slow down the process. Sometimes the results of the frame shift take longer because there's something new coming that you aren't aware of yet. Again, I experienced this while writing this very chapter.

The initial outline I had for this chapter had an idea on how to explain framing. When I tried to write on that idea, after shifting frames multiple times, the content still wasn't flowing. While taking a break and checking my global frame of certainty, I had a breakthrough. What followed was a new understanding of framing. Something I had never thought of before was revealed.

The reason the frame shifting didn't work immediately was because I needed to have that breakthrough thought before the new content started flowing. You are reading the result of that recent breakthrough right now.

In a matter of seconds, you can shift to a higher frequency. But as with everything else, the ultimate timeline is up to the process of life. Trusting the process, even during delays, removes resistance and creates ease and flow.

If you are not experiencing the immediate results of a frame shift, it is because:

1. Life needs more time to bring you what you want.
2. You have a contradicting frame you are not aware of.
3. There's something greater coming that you have yet to discover.

Stick with it. Get curious about the process. To increase the speed of the process, enjoy it. Take the time to savor it. Rushing slows the process. Appreciating it accelerates progress.

HOW OFTEN SHOULD YOU SHIFT YOUR FRAME?

Shifting frames is the process of getting into alignment. Ask yourself: *How often do I want to be in alignment?* If you're like me, you want to have the most amazing life experience and always want to be in alignment. Shift your frame before you do everything. It literally only takes a moment.

A few examples of frame-shifting opportunities:

- Before you head into the next client call, focus your awareness on having an amazing meeting with the client. As soon as you sense the awareness of that moment, you've shifted your frame.
- Before you sit down to write a powerful email, focus your awareness on an amazing, clear, completed email. You can even add a second frame and hold the awareness that you had a great time writing the email and learned something in the process.

Stacking frames fine-tunes your frequency. Maximize your results by taking the time to select the specifics you desire. Tailor your reality to the moment by stacking frames with purposeful intention.

When I create my programs and courses, I start from a frame in which the courses are going to have a positive impact on my clients while also transforming me. As a result, that continues to be my experience.

Chapter Ten

COMMON AREAS OF MISALIGNMENT

When I look at the clients that I've coached over the years, specifically those who have achieved amazing success and growth, I find a distinction that may be surprising. I have not helped any of them create success. All I have done is help remove their resistance to success.

Success is the natural state of an infinite being living in an attraction-based universe. My role is to help people embrace that reality. I cannot make someone tap into their infinite nature while they still believe they are limited.

Doing the impossible is not something you *make* happen. It is something you *allow* to happen. Resistance is the main obstacle to expanding possibility. Removing resistance is essential to doing the impossible.

I hope you are starting to understand and experience the power of the process. I hope you have begun to operate with certainty, even when details are unknown. I hope you are starting to live in active creation instead of being trapped in reaction. I hope you are learning to trust life and work with ease and flow. I hope you are, consciously or unconsciously, starting to remove resistance.

Let's continue on our journey to greatness, moving beyond struggle by framing obstacles as gateways to growth and transformation.

THE UNIVERSE IS MATHEMATICAL

Worthiness is not a requirement for receiving what you want.

The universe is mathematical. Amazing and mind-boggling, this swirl of energy and matter runs on perfectly designed systems. Let's review and expand. Like attracts like. There is alignment or misalignment. You are either a frequency match to a target or not. You are either in alignment with what you want or not. The universe does not judge or withhold reward based on merit or worthiness.

Your power is beyond comprehension. As an infinite being made of pure energy, you dictate your experience of life. You are the lens through which life flows. You are either allowing the flow of life or you are blocking it.

Doing the impossible does not require hard work, putting in the time, waking up at 5:00 a.m., taking cold showers, or yelling at the top of your lungs. The only requirements are engagement, alignment, and action.

DO YOU WANT MORE MONEY?

Let's see how open you are. Pretend you are walking down the street. A man walks up to you and says, "Hello. I'm a billionaire, and I have more money than I know what to do with. I'm good at reading people, and I can tell you are a good-hearted person. I would like to give you $50,000." He reaches in his pocket and pulls out a stack of cash.

As he holds it out to you, what is your first reaction? Would you accept it? Would you say, "Thank you" and embrace this amazing gift? Or would you react with suspicion and say, "What's the catch?" Maybe you would feel so unworthy that you would refuse it completely.

Most people will probably be resistant to accepting $50,000 for nothing. Why? It goes back to our beliefs about money and our financial identity.

Most people believe you must work to make money and will only be rewarded for your exact output. We are conditioned to accept our earnings as a direct result of our worth and skills. When we hold those beliefs, there is no room for a reality where money flows to us easily. In this universe, anything can happen in the next moment. Walking down the street and having a billionaire hand you $50,000 as a gift is not a likely situation. It is also not impossible.

Let's flip this scenario. Imagine you are a billionaire, and you make $1 billion a day. You have more money than you know what to do with and could buy everything you want and still never run out of money. When you're done buying everything you can think of, you start giving money away in order to help other people. Think of all the people in your life you would love to help. If you walked up to those people and handed them $50,000, would they easily accept it? Even after you explain how much you have, would some of them still refuse the gift?

We are conditioned to see ourselves as unworthy. Money is a worshipped and needed resource, yet we believe we are unworthy of having it. We limit ourselves, repeating this condition subconsciously: *The only way to get money is by working really hard.*

Maybe you've taken it to extremes as I did, putting further restrictions on financial success. Maybe you've added other conditions, telling yourself: *Waking up at 5:00 a.m. and taking cold showers every day is essential to financial success.* Grinding against life, trying to move ourselves into a place of worthiness denies our infinite, unlimited nature and is frankly screwed up.

By telling ourselves we must struggle and sacrifice to deserve this needed resource makes it so. Inadvertently, believing we must suffer to become worthy of having money tells the universe to bring us that reality.

Basically, we are resisting financial alignment because of socially conditioned self-judgment. It is completely backward and honestly troubling. We are focusing most of our time on the part of the process that has nothing to do with getting the result. Worth has nothing to do with it. The key is alignment.

BREAKING FREE: THE POWER OF SOCIAL CONDITIONING AND THE IMPACT IT HAS ON YOUR LIFE

You are the product of your environment, just like I am the product of my environment. Your environmental conditioning is your biggest limiting factor. Certainly your environmental conditioning has a ton of positive effects. Functioning in society, maintaining relationships, forming interests, and engaging in activities that bring you joy are just a few of those benefits. But we are not talking about why you are great right now. We are talking about what is holding you back.

As a society, we have agreed-upon rules and expectations about how life works. We think we have to work hard to make money. We think a college degree is a requirement for financial success. We think we need to be a good person to get married. Though these expectations may be true to the experiences of some people, they are not universal truths. Our belief in them—not their inherent truth—make them absolutes in our lives. When you start to understand your biggest obstacle to alignment is your conditioning, you can begin to move beyond these limiting conditions and remove resistance to success.

When you review all the reasons you don't have what you want or why you haven't reached your desired level of success, how much of that is based on excuses or emotions? Probably most of it.

There are areas of your life where you hit the limits of your social conditioning, and you've pushed beyond them. You may have become amazing in a specific area despite outside opinions and conditions. You may have become the black sheep of your family by breaking through your socially accepted family norms. Even if all of that is true to your life experience, I bet you have other areas where you've struggled for years, trying to burst through ludicrous social norms.

How we feel when we come up against these fictitious blocks to success stagnates our momentum. But it is all artificial. Pushing through the façade and expanding beyond what is "acceptable" can be uncomfortable. So we avoid the quest for what we want because uncertainty is scary. This is the human journey in the late 20th and early 21st centuries. I've been there. I know what it's like. The good news is you can set yourself free from the artificial cage of your social conditioning.

THE HUMAN JOURNEY IS EMOTIONAL

Being a human in a mathematical universe is a challenging journey because human existence is not calculated. It is emotional. It is full of ups and downs, twists and turns, misunderstandings, and trial and error. Our identity is created by so many outside factors that connect to who we truly are can sometimes seem impossible, bleak, or pointless. Especially when our individual, invaluable guidance systems (our emotions) are portrayed as problematic by culture and society.

When we are struggling to accept who we are, it can be highly beneficial to pinpoint what part of that struggle is based in what society tells us we should be. My journey to becoming a coach led me to explore my relationship with social conditioning and beliefs, especially around emotion. My destiny was to discover how to get what I want, how to create my own reality, and, most importantly, how to feel the way I want to feel. But first I had to come to terms with who I am, beyond what I have been conditioned to believe I should be.

From a young age, I always felt a lot. My dad called me his "sensitive boy."

Growing up in a "tough it out" culture, I thought something was wrong with me and my intense feelings. This disconnect between what I felt and what I was supposed to feel created resistance to accepting and embracing myself as I was.

As the black sheep of the family, I could see that there was something different about me. My mom, dad, and sister are all comfortable following the model of getting a job, filling a specified role, and toeing the line.

Even as a child, I was always doing things my own way, which was a point of contention with my parents and caused me to rebel. In my early 20s, drinking became a way to numb my unwanted intense feelings. Overcoming these obstacles and working through misguided solutions was vital to finding my unique path.

Looking back, I know there was nothing wrong with me. I know those emotions were an important indicator of my passion. Born highly empathetic and intuitive, I am innately in tune with reading emotions from other people, which can be overwhelming.

Feeling all these emotions, I thought they were all my own. But they were actually the emotions of the people around me combined with my emotions. Now I understand that I truly am different from my family and many other people in that way. After perceiving my ability as a liability for decades, I now know my gift for feeling intensely and reading other people's emotions is something I was destined to share with my clients and the world.

I share this story to show that accepting ourselves—all of ourselves—enables our unique gifts to come to light. Your human journey is specifically yours. Share it with the world by embracing what makes you unique. Denying parts of who we are because of social conditioning is no way to live your life.

YOUR UNIQUE PATH

Every person's path is distinct and dynamic. But all of us are on a journey of creation and exploration. This is why we are here. We are not here to be perfect. We are not here to be robots. Societal messages and norms may tell us we need to strive for perfection and take a specific path. But in every moment lies the choice to rise above all socially conditioned limitations and accept our true fate—endless possibility.

While traveling our path, we look to others for guidance. It is a natural instinct. But how often does this create self-judgment because the paths of others are different from our own? When we look at others' achievements, we often feel unworthy because we are focused on what we have yet to accomplish.

Seeking the guidance of a mentor has its benefits, but it will not reveal your distinct path. Copying the success models of other people ignores your unique mission. Have you ever copied another person's success model and it didn't work? I have. I switched my career to try to copy someone else's path. I thought if I could be like them, I would be successful. It wasn't until I quit trying to be them and started following my own knowing that I found my unique path to success.

Why is that? It's simple. There is no one like you. There is only one you. There is only one me. There is no other combination of energy and matter in this universe exactly like each of us. You are as distinct as your fingerprints. Knowing that, how can you believe your journey needs to follow someone else's path?

When we follow and trust our own unique path, we find our greatest success. Following someone else's path will lead you to mediocre success at best. You'll never stand out from the crowd following another person's tracks.

My life is an example of this truth. I left a good job to become a life coach. Everybody thought I was nuts. The average life coach in the United States makes $35,000 a year, basically 25 percent of what I was making in tech sales. Why in the world would I want to leave a "good-paying job" and take a 75 percent pay cut?

From the outside, my path didn't make any sense. Your unique path may not make sense to the people around you either, especially at the beginning. But it will make sense to you because of the way it makes you feel.

Before I found my path, I was driven solely by my desire for success and plagued by the fear that I couldn't make it happen. At this moment, your path may not be clear. And it may not present itself in an instant the way mine did because *your path is unique*. Whether you have found your passion or not, stop listening to what everyone else says you should do and start following what *you know* you should do.

BEYOND SELF-JUDGMENT

Self-judgment is another form of misalignment. It is misalignment with yourself. Usually based on our social conditioning, it occurs when we focus on what we think *should* be happening. Let's look at ourselves objectively and recognize self-judgement for what it really is. Self-judgment is the pattern of labeling our unwanted results.

You are on a journey of growth and exploration. Right and wrong are labels created by social conditioning. Instead of looking at right and wrong, let's look at your past and present as a series of results.

When we don't achieve the results we want, we need to understand why. We tell ourselves the unwanted results are bad. We tell ourselves that we are bad. The truth is we simply can't see the big picture. At this time, we don't have the perspective to see that we need that specific result.

Most likely you have learned something much more valuable from "bad" experiences than you have from the "good" ones. We need those inspiring experiences, though they may be painful, because they stretch and prepare us for achieving future success.

The road to creating world-changing results is lined with perceived failures. When you feel self-judgment, remind yourself that all parts of your path are necessary. All results are the process of life in action, not an indicator that you are bad or unworthy.

Another way to give yourself liberation from self-judgment is to give yourself permission to do your best. Remember you are human, not a robot. Every moment of every day, you are doing the best you can. Some days you perform exceptionally well. Other days you perform poorly. Put that variance into perspective. Your best is different depending on the day. This contradicts our social conditioning that tells us we should be perfect every single day. Doing the impossible has nothing to do with being perfect.

We are here for the journey and to experience the process of life, which, by nature, is a series of ups and downs. Stop wasting energy and move out of self-judgment. I guarantee every moment prior to now you did the best you could. When you look back, it is easy to see better options. But in the moment, you maximized the information you had at the time.

There was never a moment when you made a decision with the intent of screwing up your life. You were never given these two options:

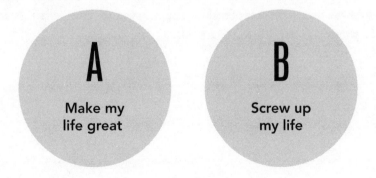

You never intentionally chose option B. There may have been a situation in your life when you knew there was option A, and you went with option B. That choice was not a failure. At the time, you were simply incapable of executing option A. Life happened the only way it could.

The moments from your past that elicit self-judgment, most likely, included interactions with other people. Your behavior in those situations is a mathematical result. It was the sum of the energies of those involved. You may have been playing a role to help give another infinite being a gift in life they desperately needed. A gift only you could deliver through the behavior determined by the process of life.

There are an infinite number of ways you can judge yourself and your past behavior. But one thing is certain: The past is fixed. You can call it good, or you can call it bad. It's your choice. I suggest simply calling it the past.

To get out of the past and into the future, give yourself permission to do your best and remember your best is different depending on the day. Give yourself permission to be human. Spend your time focusing on the future by not dwelling on the past. The way you get out of the never-ending spiral of self-judgment is to stop playing the game.

Love yourself for everything you are. And love yourself for everything you are not. Meet and accept yourself in this present moment because you cannot change it. You are exactly where you are meant to be.

What you can change is the next moment. The best way to change the next moment is to be balanced and aligned. It's much easier to create amazing things in balance, versus starting in a hole of self-judgment and unworthiness. Let go of the labels you have put on the past and allow yourself to be human. Embrace the infinite being you are. Feel the emotions of the journey you've been given. Accept all results as a necessary part of making you who you are destined to become.

Keep moving forward. You've got this.

Chapter Eleven
THE PROCESS OF LIFE

As you progress through this book, I hope you are noticing yourself shift into new frames with each chapter. I hope you can feel yourself moving into better alignment.

Questions to check your progress:

- Are you beginning to view things from a new perspective?
- Are you starting to think about things differently?
- Are certainty and confidence increasing?

This book is designed specifically to shift your global frame of life. The wonderful truth about this content is that there is always another level of understanding. The more you engage with these ideas, the more you get out of the content. Now, let's continue on to a greater level of alignment.

The next part of doing the impossible is following the process of life. I know this sounds oversimplified and almost ridiculous, but it is an invaluable component of doing the impossible. The process of life is why you are on the planet at this exact moment. Aligning yourself with the process of life is how you live life on your terms and create the reality of your dreams.

You have done the best you can to follow the process of life up until now. That said, let's further expand your understanding of how life works. First, there are only three reasons you don't have something you want:

1. You have resistance (misalignment) to the process of getting it.
2. You have resistance (misalignment) to having it.
3. Life needs more time to bring it to you.

First, alignment with the process of life is just as important as alignment with what you want. To hit your target, your individual process of life will include one of these growth areas to prepare you for achieving your target: stretching who you are to become who you need to be, learning something you need to know, or mastering a skill you need to utilize. Most likely it is a combination of all three.

The second reason you might not have what you want relates to your identity. You may need to get into alignment with having your desired result. As discussed, my financial identity kept me from success for years. Identifying ourselves as innately worthy and shedding the restraints of social conditioning better aligns us with the success we desire.

Lastly, if you are aligned with the process and your success identity but still aren't getting the result, life simply needs more time to bring it to you. In that situation, your task is to stay aligned. You job is to take action while trusting that life is working for you, not against you.

YOUR INTERNAL GUIDANCE SYSTEM

You may be asking, "How do I follow the *process of life*? Am I not doing that just by being alive?" Well, no. Only if you are following your guidance system are you following the process of life.

Your internal guidance system is a complete network that, like your frame and mindset, is always running and supplying information. Through feelings, thoughts, and naturally inspired ideas, your internal guidance system is constantly giving you input from life. The guidance system is your emotions.

Emotions are not unwanted, out-of-control energy sent to torment you. Emotions are valuable indicators of alignment. Use these questions to check your alignment with a target:

- Does it feel good, or does it feel bad?
- Does it feel exciting, or does it feel boring?
- Do you feel inspired to take massive action, or would you just rather avoid it, sit on your butt, and procrastinate?

If you feel good (positive emotion), you are in alignment. If you feel bad (negative emotion), you are in misalignment.

We are conditioned to think having emotions is a bad thing. But your emotions are how you interact with the world. They are how you *feel* the world.

When you dial into your emotions and embrace them as positive and useful, even when they feel negative, they become a powerful tool. When you trust the input from your internal guidance system and practice utilizing that input, your intuition becomes a sixth sense. It becomes a superpower. We have access to this vital information all the time. Instead of avoiding your emotions, harness their power by knowing they bring invaluable insight.

IS YOUR THINKING OUT OF CONTROL?

If you live in the Western world as I do, your thinking is probably out of control. Which is simultaneously funny and sad to say because it's so true.

Your thinking interrupts your guidance system. Your thinking tells you to question your emotions. Do phrases like, *I shouldn't be feeling this way* or *Don't get emotional* pass through your head when emotion arises? We've heard people say things like that to themselves and others so much that we start to say them to ourselves. Maybe we have even said things like that to other people.

Trying to control our emotions is misguided and highly problematic. Accepting the process of life shifts our focus from trying to master our emotions to learning how to master the integration of our emotions. Why not utilize all the information you have access to? Why immediately rule out the insight of your intuition?

Don't ignore your internal guidance system. Use it. Don't let social conditioning silence your knowing.

Oh, that dreaded social conditioning is coming up again. Do you see how much it affects us? We are ruled by social conditioning. *Do what you're supposed to do. Do what everybody says you should do.* Programmed thoughts such as these are the major enemy of your internal guidance system. They block you from accurately interpreting your emotions. And sadly, they aren't even really your thoughts.

When I look at all the success I've experienced over the past two years—growing my business by ten times, doubling my income multiple times, building an amazing team around me—I know none of it would've happened if I had followed my thinking. It happened because I followed my *knowing*.

Your knowing is the information produced by your internal guidance system.

It is much more powerful than your thinking. The problem is we don't listen to it, because we have been programmed to try to ignore it. We question our knowing because it contradicts our thinking.

If your thinking could lead you through doing the impossible, you would already have all you desire. I'm sure you've spent plenty of time trying to think your way into accelerated success. I know I have. Your thinking alone is never going to conquer the impossible. If you want to do the impossible, you have to follow your knowing. That is where the magic happens. Get aligned with your knowing, and find trust and faith in that journey. Again, align yourself with the process of life.

How do you move into alignment with the process of life? How do you use your knowing to do the impossible? It's simple. Shift into a frame that embraces the process of life without fear, and hold the awareness of that future version of you that follows your knowing. That's it.

To experience an amazing life filled with magic and wonder, you have to go against what you've been taught and let go of trying to figure out success. Your thinking does not create accelerated growth and success. Wild, impactful synchronicities and magic connections with new people enable big expansion to come from the unknown. Only your knowing (internal guidance system) can lead you in the unknown. This is exactly what I tell all my clients. Follow your knowing and execute with your thinking.

HOW TO TELL THE DIFFERENCE BETWEEN YOUR THINKING AND YOUR KNOWING?

The simplest way to tell the difference between your thinking and your knowing is to ask yourself a question. Pay attention to how long it takes the answer to come. If the answer pops up immediately, almost cutting off the question, that is your knowing. Answers produced by your thinking take more time. Knowing answers are instinctive because they come from your gut instinct. They don't require processing time like the brain does.

The other way to know the difference between your knowing and your thinking is to sit with your question. Your knowing is that persistent inner truth that nags you and won't go away. Follow that guidance and accept that it won't always make sense to your thinking.

On a coaching call with one of my amazing clients, I asked, "What's the most important thing you could do today?" He answered quickly, "Get a massage." It was a surprising answer, and I got the sense that the client was surprised that getting a massage would be the most important thing to do. But since I knew the answer came from his knowing, I suggested he get a massage.

Not only did he get a massage, he started getting weekly massages. Now the time he spends getting a massage is one of his most productive and highest-earning hours of the week. During that time, he comes up with amazing ideas. Those ideas have led to exciting business opportunities, growth in income, new resources, and overall expansion in his life and business. All because he followed his knowing and did something that from the outside might have seemed illogical or unimportant.

To identify your thinking, ask yourself one of the following questions:

- What am I supposed to do right now?
- What does everyone else think I should do?

Those questions are guaranteed to generate a socially conditioned (thinking) answer.

CERTAINTY VS. UNCERTAINTY: THE KEY TO FRAME ALIGNMENT

Certainty is a feeling based on something known or proven to be true. Uncertainty is the feeling based on something not known or unreliable. When we do something we've never done before, we often default to uncertainty because we don't know *exactly* how to hit the target. Though uncertainty is a completely natural reaction, it can make executing extremely, and unnecessarily, difficult. Operating from certainty, even when we are facing something new, aligns us with our target. When you operate in certainty, you have a clear frame. That clear frame gives life a clear frequency to respond to.

We are conditioned to believe that certainty comes from success or experience. When we are successful and experienced at something, we know exactly what to do. We have confidence, which creates a clear, certain frame around producing a result. Life responds to that frame and gives you what you want. You may think it happened because of your expertise. But it wasn't your expertise that delivered the desired result. It was your frame of certainty.

Remember, we are socially conditioned to believe that there is only one truth. Now that you know this belief is limiting and you understand that truth is based on perspective, let's expand your relationship with truth.

From this moment on, know—with certainty—you choose your own truth. You choose what you believe, which means you can decide to be certain even when you have no idea what to do. You can choose to be in a clear aligned frame with your target even when the way to execute is still unclear. That is how to live in active creation. That is how you master the art of reshaping your reality.

How do we get out of uncertainty? Again, you shift your frame. Can you imagine a version of you at some point in the future who knows exactly how to hit that impossible target?

When you think of a big target, you may be concerned, fixated, or even obsessed with knowing the details of how you will hit the mark. Instead of wasting energy trying to figure out how the process of life will bring you the result, shift your frame. Can you get a sense of that future version of you who knows how to execute? Hold the awareness of that version for ten seconds. Pay attention to what happens to your certainty.

Uncertainty is an indicator. When we are uncertain, our internal guidance system is telling us to refocus and shift our awareness. That feeling of uncertainty isn't a problem. It's a signal. Use the information produced by your emotional reaction to get out of reaction and into active creation. Don't let fear distract you and make you forget that all emotions are there to help you.

The same thing goes for doubt. Doubt is also an indicator that it's time to shift frames. Doubt is an indicator that you have access to a higher frame. Doubt is not a problem, just as a notification or signal is not a problem. It's just information when we view it as such. Stop reacting to the information and start letting it guide you.

PAST MODELS OF SUCCESS ARE LIMITATIONS, NOT ACCELERATORS

Reviewing other performance coaching methodologies, you may find a focus on modeling future success on past success. Those programs are designed to anchor your old model of success so that you can duplicate it. It is logical to use the same process that created success five years ago to create success now, if you want to stay at the same level. But if you want to level up, that is simply not how life works.

Old success models don't help you achieve accelerated growth and expansion, because you're not the same person you were when those models worked. Each day you are more than you were the day before. Therefore, using past models to create future success limits potential.

Once, years ago, I was on a call with a client who wanted to make more progress than he was experiencing at the time. He said, "I know I can do it. I've done it before. I know if I wake up at 5:00 a.m., I'll get the result. Because every time I've woken up at 5:00 a.m., I always got the result." This may sound like a breakthrough and a clear indicator to the path to success. While waking up at 5:00 a.m. may help achieve this client's goal, it also limits possibility.

If you believe that waking up at 5:00 a.m. is a requirement for success, you also believe you cannot hit your target unless you wake up at 5:00 a.m. Remember, we need to be careful with our beliefs because the inverse is also true. Such subtle inverse beliefs put conditions on our capability and capacity and deny the unlimited nature of life.

How can you move beyond past models of success that are limiting you? Be open to anything happening next. Remove all conditions for success. Allow success to come from any direction at any time.

Let's get into alignment.

Repeat After Me (out loud):

- *I take full ownership of my life and everything in it.*
- *From this moment on, I choose to live in a reality where I am free from all rules and prerequisites for success.*
- *Success can come from any direction, at any time.*
- *Success can come from any person, anything, at any time.*
- *I take full ownership of any memories, beliefs, and experiences that are contradictory to this, and I integrate all of them now.*
- *I choose to believe this 100 percent, past, present, and future—all versions of me. And I take full ownership of everything contradictory to this and integrate all of it now.*

THE PROBLEM WITH WANTING

As we've covered previously, like attracts like in our attraction-based universe. At the same time, it is important to remember that all timeframes are contingent on the process of life. When we are waiting on life to deliver, we need to avoid slipping into a state of wanting.

For example, I could align myself with becoming a billionaire. Though I am in perfect alignment with that desire, the process of life will determine how long it will take me to become a billionaire. Predictably, it will not happen overnight.

We must allow life to move things around on its own timeline. Trusting the process of life allows life to deliver what we want, but not necessarily *when* we want it. If our trust falters due to impatience, we may find ourselves in wanting.

At the beginning of every mission, you have something you want to accomplish or receive. Wanting is a necessary, basic human instinct. We all do it. The distinction is we need to avoid remaining in a state of wanting. Staying in wanting, paradoxically and sometimes confusingly, places us in misalignment with what we want.

Operating from a present state of wanting is embracing the *lack* of the thing you want. Life responds to what you are in this moment, not what you want to be. If you spend every day walking around repetitively saying and thinking, *I want more money,* you are basically asking life to continue your experience of not having enough money. Erroneously aligning yourself with the lack of what you want puts you in misalignment with your target.

The secret is to become what you want, and life will deliver. Framing instantly transforms you into what you want. By mastering framing and trusting the process of life, no matter how long it takes to deliver, you can begin to easily align yourself with what you want and stop living in wanting. You will move from a state of wanting into a state of abundance, which attracts abundance.

Wanting is a misunderstanding of how life works. Most often originating from a frame of uncertainty, wanting contradicts the belief that you will receive everything that you are a match to. Don't spend time in wanting. Be a creator. Align with what you want, trust and enjoy the process of life, and watch in wonder as it delivers.

PICK THE RIGHT STARTING POINT

One technique that will radically transform your level of success is picking the right starting point (the correct frame). That ideal starting point is beyond reaction to your present reality. Remember, your current life situation is what it is. It cannot be changed. Your current life situation is a result of the past, not an indicator of the future. Don't make decisions out of reaction to your present life situation.

Make your decisions based on where you are going, not where you have been. Start in success by deciding, with 100 percent certainty, the result will happen. That is the quickest and easiest way to get into alignment.

Before you begin crafting your strategy and taking action, tell yourself: *This is the result I'm going to achieve. I believe this with 100 percent certainty.* This shifts your frame into alignment and sets your frequency to match the target.

Next, utilize your knowing to create strategy, and start taking action. Remain flexible as you execute with your thinking. Trusting the process of life is more valuable than sticking to your strategy.

LET EXCITEMENT BE YOUR GUIDE

Excitement is our most powerful emotion. It is the clearest indicator for finding your unique path. When you are excited, life is saying, "This is going to fill you with more excitement, joy, and passion. Go do this now!" That is a clear message. We spend so much time trying to figure out life, often ignoring the most important messages within ourselves, such as excitement.

Follow your excitement. There is a reason life is using it to get your attention. It's the best sign of your knowing. And, most likely, the reason you haven't followed your excitement in the past is because your thinking told you it was wrong or stupid or that other people wouldn't accept your decision.

Now you are operating from a frame that knows the truth. You know life works in amazing ways when we follow our knowing and execute with our thinking. Let life guide you. Follow your excitement into the world of unbounded possibility.

Let's get into alignment. Answer these questions:
- Do you understand that your emotions are a part of your guidance system?
- Are you ready to start following your guidance system instead of reacting to it?
- Are you ready to shorten your path to success?

Now let's integrate.

Repeat After Me (out loud):

- *I take full ownership of my life and everything in it.*
- *I take full ownership of my past, present, and future.*
- *I understand that life is a process.*
- *I understand that I am guided, and my emotions are a form of guidance.*
- *I understand that emotions are to be followed and interpreted, not ignored.*
- *I choose to become more aware of when I'm operating in uncertainty.*
- *I choose to easily allow myself to feel certainty, even when I don't know what to do, even when I'm operating in the unknown.*
- *I choose to learn from my past models of success when appropriate, but never be limited by them.*
- *I take full ownership of any past models of success that are limiting me now, and I release all of them now.*
- *I choose to live in a reality where I am open to all new models of success.*
- *I choose to live in a reality where alignment is my default state.*
- *I choose to live in a reality where success flows to me with ease.*
- *I choose to live in a reality where money flows to me with ease.*
- *I choose to believe this 100 percent, past, present, and future—all versions of me. And I immediately take ownership of anything contradictory to this and integrate all of it now.*

Frame-Shifting Exercise

- Can you get a sense of a future version of you that understands your emotions at a greater level than you do now?
- Can you imagine a version of you in the future that is fully aligned with your emotional guidance system?
- Can you get a sense of a future version of you that enjoys following your excitement as a key indicator of intuition?

Great. Hold your awareness on that version of you for ten seconds. How do you feel now?

Chapter Twelve

OBSTACLES: THE GATEWAYS TO TRANSFORMATION

In case you haven't figured it out by now, the process of doing the impossible is actually the process of transforming who you are. To do the impossible, you need to be willing to become more than you are now. You need to become a version of yourself that is in alignment with doing the impossible. This is the most authentic and unlimited version of you, and the real result of the process is alignment with that frequency. Hitting the big impossible target is simply a byproduct.

THE BOAT HOIST

When your excitement is guiding you to something you can't afford, it means a path to affording it is presently unfolding.

Recently I came up with two ideas for Jason Drees Coaching that will triple our revenue in six months. And it all began with a boat hoist.

My family and I moved to Texas from California a few months ago. We have a great time boating together. So when we moved, we brought our twenty-foot Sea-Doo boat with us. In California, our boat was the perfect size. However, after taking it out near our new home in Texas, it became clear that we might need a bigger boat for enjoying our local waterway, Lake Travis.

Lake Travis has more traffic than we're used to, which makes for a rougher ride in a boat the size of ours. But we like going to Lake Travis because it is fifteen minutes from our house. I found a dry stack parking space at a local marina. I call before we leave the house, and the marina takes my boat out of the stack and puts it in the water. When we get there, it's ready to go. It's perfect.

After a month of boating on Lake Travis, I began researching bigger boats. The problem with getting a bigger boat is having a space to store it. My current dry stack parking space will not hold a boat larger than twenty-two feet, and I was considering a boat between twenty-four and twenty-six feet.

Deciding I couldn't let the need for a new storage space hold me back, I reached out to the marina to find a twenty-eight-foot slip that would be available soon. (If you aren't familiar, a boat slip is like a parking spot for a boat.) Finding a slip was great news. The catch was the spot included a 10,000-pound boat hoist, which increased the cost of the spot significantly. A boat hoist is a mechanism installed underwater that suspends a docked boat out of the water and enables dry storage, as well as easier access to the lake. Considering how much we enjoy being on the lake, the boat hoist would be a great thing to have—but I didn't even have the new boat yet. After hearing the price of this premium spot, I initially moved on. For some reason, I couldn't stop thinking about the slip and the boat hoist. I knew at some point, maybe a few years from now, we would have a bigger boat and a slip on Lake Travis, but I didn't think it was necessary now.

Over the next few weeks, I heard multiple people say, "You got a slip on Lake Travis? How did you do that? It's normally a two-to-three-year wait." My wife had someone tell her the same thing. When I hear something like that, I pay attention because I see it as synchronicity.

Unknowingly, we had somehow cut to the front of a waitlist for something

I didn't think we needed yet. My interest increased. My rational mind and my wife were telling me to wait, but it felt like life was telling me the time was now.

I continued to get more excited about the boat hoist. I called the marina with the limit of spending $2,500 on the hoist. When they told me it was $10,000, I said that was too much and tried to move on from my excitement.

After a few days, I still couldn't stop thinking about it. I told my wife, "I don't know why, but I'm really excited about it. I can't stop thinking about it." She said, "It's silly, but I know you are going to do what you are going to do." (Not the first time she had said that to me.) I called the marina and offered $8,500 for the boat hoist, thinking it would be rejected. I told myself: *I've made an attempt, and when they say they won't accept that price, I can be at peace about it.* But they accepted the offer, saying, "Sold. It's yours." (I later found out that the hoist needed $1,000 of updates to hold my boat. So it had turned into a $9,500 investment.)

What is the point of the story? Stick with me.

After I made the deal, I woke up in the middle the night. I couldn't go back to sleep. I was overwhelmed with worry because we were planning to buy a new home in the next six months and would need money for a down payment. Traditional thinking (social conditioning) would tell me not to spend almost $10,000 on something I didn't need six months before buying a new house.

My thoughts were racing, and I was asking myself, *What am I doing? Why did I just buy a $10,000 parking space for a boat I don't even have yet?* I was telling myself, *I am writing a book that no one's going read. I'm doing a live event, and no one's going to show up.* As old fears crept in, I was overwhelmed by visions of failure.

Then I remembered a conversation I had with one of the JDC coaches, Ben Austin. During that conversation he had said, "It's not about you." When he said that, it resonated with me in a different context. But as I was lying awake, my subconscious mind threw that phrase back at me, and it revealed something more. I could hear Ben's voice in my head say, "It's not about you." And I realized I was focusing on the wrong thing. I was focusing on my experience of life, as opposed to focusing on my life experience.

When I reflect on my life and my recent accelerated success as a whole, the timing of the boat hoist makes perfect sense. My life experience is aligned with skipping the waitlist and buying the boat hoist because today I maintain a frequency match to continued growth and increased income. The moment I stopped focusing on my experience of life (the way I felt lying awake) and started focusing my life experience (my life as whole), the doubt, worry, and fear disappeared.

That's when I realized I had been following my excitement about the boat hoist. I realized that judging my excitement was wrong. I decided to go all in. I committed to the path of being the creator of my reality. I also realized that if I didn't buy the boat hoist, I would be operating in a frame of scarcity. Denying the synchronicity would be implying that I would not have enough money for the down payment on the house.

After my midnight breakthrough, I decided to no longer judge my excitement by reshaping my reality. Reminding myself that anything can happen in the next moment and money can come from anywhere at any time, I released all judgment of myself for following my excitement and went back to sleep with ease.

The next day, I decided to launch a ten-member mastermind program. I don't remember how the idea came up, but I remember being excited about it. I knew it would be successful because the groups I had been working with were creating amazing results. Immediately I got to work with my team to release the program application. Within ten days, I had twenty-five applicants.

This series of inspiring decisions also impacted my company's live events program. The same day I came up with the mastermind program, I had the idea for a three-day small group intensive to push our powerful, large group live events even further. Between the intensive and mastermind program, I created two large revenue streams that didn't exist before that breakthrough. The worry over the $9,500 seemed almost insignificant just a few days after I first identified the problem.

My excitement led me to buying a boat hoist. The boat hoist led me to waking up in the middle of the night. Being unable to fall asleep led me to shifting my frame around money, which elevated my financial frequency. That shift immediately led me to new ideas that would triple the monthly revenue of my business within ninety days, all because I followed my excitement and bought a boat hoist.

THE GATEWAY TO TRANSFORMATION

Obstacles are inherently unappealing from a conventional, socially-conditioned mindset. It can often seem like our main task as humans is attempting to avoid obstacles. We believe obstacles are problems (and simply no fun) because they can cause stress, anxiety, and fear.

However, what if obstacles were no longer a source of stress and headaches? What happens when we realize that our perception of obstacles is the real source of stress?

Obstacles are defined as things that hinder progress. But from my perspective, obstacles actually encourage progress. We label something an obstacle because it is new and different compared to situations we have conquered before. So moving past an obstacle doesn't have to be scary and stressful when we know the only requirement is doing something new or different or becoming something new and different.

When taking on an obstacle, we have to stretch to become a new version of ourselves. We need a different, elevated frame of operation. Obstacles demand a higher frequency. We should be grateful for obstacles because they are opportunities for transformation. They push us to the next level. Don't you love the results of the next level?

Surprise! The negative emotions you feel when hitting obstacles are not the problem. The stress and discomfort are your guidance system indicating you are up against the limits of your current frame. Our emotional reaction to an obstacle is an alert saying, "Go beyond your comfort zone. You have outgrown this frame."

We can't rely on old patterns to solve a new obstacle. A breakthrough is required. When our guidance system sends an alert (fear) that we are at maximum capacity, it's time to push the pedal down and level up. After a breakthrough, our guidance system will recalibrate at the new level. But those moments between shifting hold the most resistance.

If you are operating from a frame of growth and expansion, you can more objectively witness your emotional guidance system stretching. You can see negative emotions as valuable indicators that you are about to shift frames.

It's like driving a manual transmission car at sixty miles an hour in fourth gear. The car is loud. Vibrations are high. It feels like everything is going to fall apart. It feels like you should slow down and ease off the gas. Unless you are an experienced manual driver. Then you know the intensity is telling you to shift into fifth gear. The second you shift into fifth gear, all of the symptoms of misalignment disappear.

Back to the boat hoist. When this new opportunity (obstacle) began to cause stress, I knew it was an indicator of growth. I knew that life would not bring me excitement about something I couldn't afford without a way to pay for it. My job was to transform into the new version of myself that knew what to do. The boat hoist was the catalyst for creating new revenue streams and fortifying my belief that obstacles are the gateways to transformation.

What if you adopted this frame? What if you embraced every obstacle as a gateway to transformation? If growth and expansion are why we are on this planet and obstacles are inherently growth opportunities, obstacles become the real target. Start to see obstacles for what they are—indicators that you are approaching an on-ramp to an elevated frame.

What becomes possible when you see every obstacle is an opportunity for growth?

EMBRACE HITTING YOUR LIMITS

Doing the impossible will push you, challenge you, and drive you to your limits. Life gives us accelerated, amazing results when we are operating at a level that can handle them. To accelerate your expansion with ease and flow, embrace everything along the way and be open to the journey required for making the impossible possible.

Meet the impossible with the willingness to do what needs to be done, which may or may not be a lot of work. Don't let fear of work stop you from doing the impossible. Show up willing to do what it takes, and sometimes the willingness is all that is needed.

One pattern I've seen clients get stuck in is avoiding certain emotions, specifically the feeling of being overwhelmed. Who likes to feel overwhelmed? Usually accompanied by stress and anxiety, it is easy to see why we try to avoid it. Feeling overwhelmed can be terrifying, but let's look at what being overwhelmed actually is.

In our modern concept of the word, *overwhelmed* means "I have more than I can manage." I have "too much stuff." Well, I'm here to tell you that "stuff" is life. So we can also describe overwhelmed as an emotional response to "too much life."

When you are overwhelmed, everything you've done prior to now has created more life than you feel you can currently handle. Your success has grown faster than your ability to manage it. From that perspective, it sounds like a good thing. When a client says they are overwhelmed, I see a reason to celebrate.

Even though I celebrate being overwhelmed, I know it doesn't feel great. Just like driving that old stick shift in fourth gear at sixty miles an hour, being overwhelmed is intense and can be detrimental if it continues for extended periods of time. But it also can be an indicator that you have access to a higher frame. When my business grew by ten times in four months, I had to shift my frame every single day to get out of feeling overwhelmed.

Here was my process:

Three months before the expansion, I felt as if I had everything under control. Recalling this while in an active state of feeling overwhelmed from the recent growth, I went back further, and I looked at my perspective from ten years ago. That version of me would have been completely overwhelmed with my life *before* the expansion. He wasn't even capable of handling the business before it exploded, much less operating with ease and having everything under control.

In that moment, I realized there was a future version of me who would not be overwhelmed by my current expansion. One of my most powerful framing exercises came from that breakthrough.

When I feel overwhelmed, I stop and get a sense of that future version of myself. For ten seconds I hold the awareness of a future me that would know exactly what to do in my present situation. The overwhelmingness disappears instantly because I have shifted frames.

If you want to do the impossible, you have to accept everything life gives you. You are the lens through which life flows, and if you are resisting a specific emotion such as feeling overwhelmed, you are resisting the flow of life. Doing the impossible will not work when you are in resistance. You have to be open to life giving you more than you can currently handle so that you can rise to the occasion. Embrace all your obstacles as opportunities to frame shift. And now that you know the truth, you can shift frames in seconds. Doing the impossible truly is that easy.

Welcome to a Life of Creation

Welcome to life on your terms. You now have all the tools you need to do the impossible and create (and savor) the reality you truly desire.

Here are some quick tips to keep you centered and aligned while navigating the day-to-day:

1. Your starting point matters. Pick the right starting point.
2. To remain in alignment, frame shift before everything you do.
3. Follow the process of life with love and acceptance. See everything that comes up as part of your unique path.
4. Embrace obstacles. This relieves stress and accelerate transformation.
5. Savor the process. You will be amazed. Life is designed to work for you.

If you ever feel lost, ask yourself: *Am I living a life of reaction? Or am I living a life of creation?*

Live without limits. They only exist in your mind. Life wants to flow through you. Let it flow.

Chapter Thirteen
GETTING INTO ALIGNMENT EXERCISES

Now that we've made it through the primary discourse of this book, it's time to focus on the final integration piece. This final chapter of Repeat After Me statements will complete your alignment and integration into the frequency of doing the impossible.

Let's get into alignment. Answer these questions:

- Are you ready to integrate everything you've learned so far?
- Are you ready to get into full alignment with everything you've learned so far?
- Are you ready to get into full alignment with doing the impossible?

Frame-Shifting Exercise

- Can you get a sense of a future version of you that was transformed by this chapter?
- Can you get a sense of a future version of you that easily integrated everything in this chapter?
- Can you get a sense of the future version of you that remembers reading this chapter for the first time and the powerful impact it had on your life?

Let's get into alignment with full engagement.

Repeat After Me (out loud):

- *I take full ownership of my life and everything in it.*
- *I take full ownership of my past, present, and future.*
- *I choose to be fully engaged in my life.*
- *I take full ownership of anything and everything that has ever made me want to disengage or escape from life.*
- *I release all of it now.*
- *I choose to engage fully in my life, to explore my full potential, to uncover who I really am, to discover what I'm truly capable of and dive into this magical experience of life, for the well-being of all.*
- *I choose to believe this 100 percent, past, present, and future—all versions of me. And I take ownership of anything contradictory to this and I integrate it completely now.*

Pause for three breaths

Let's get into alignment with immediate growth and transformation.

Repeat After Me (out loud):

- *I live in the world of immediate transformation.*
- *When I want to transform, I transform immediately.*
- *When I don't want to transform, I don't transform.*
- *When I want to grow and change, I automatically release blocks to my growth and change, because I am 100 percent in control of my transformation.*
- *I choose to live in a reality where the mindset tools in this book will work when I want them to work, because whether they work or not is based on my conscious decision, not my old patterns.*
- *From this moment on, I choose to live in a world of immediate transformation because I no longer want any limit on how fast or how much I can transform at one time.*
- *I choose to believe this 100 percent, past, present, and future—all versions of me. And I take ownership of anything contradictory to this, and I integrate it completely now.*

Pause for three breaths

Let's get into alignment with this book.

Repeat After Me (out loud):

- *I choose to live in a reality where this book gives me more benefits than I ever imagined, now and in the future.*
- *I choose to live in a reality where this book creates new opportunities for me to grow, expand, and connect with other amazing people.*
- *I choose to live in a reality where every time I read this book, I get more out of it.*
- *I choose to live in a reality where the concepts in this book are easy for me to understand and master, almost as if I always knew them and am remembering them now.*
- *I take ownership of any conscious or unconscious doubts I have about this book working for me, and I integrate all of it completely now.*
- *I choose to believe this 100 percent, past, present, and future—all versions of me. I take ownership of anything contradictory to this, and I integrate it completely now.*

Pause for three breaths.

Let's get into alignment with the process of life.

Repeat After Me (out loud):

- *I understand that life is a process, just like climbing a mountain.*
- *I choose to explore my unique process of life.*
- *Even though at times I may feel like rushing, I choose to understand that rushing slows down the process of life.*
- *Because if I want to climb a mountain, I can't skip any sections of it; I have to walk every step of the path.*
- *In fact, the fastest way to move through the process of life is to savor each step. Just like when I'm on vacation, time goes really fast.*

- *I choose to understand that success and failure are both parts of life.*
- *I choose to explore the process of life that is unfolding in front of me.*
- *I understand that the present is the result of the past, not an indicator of the future. I understand that anything can happen next.*
- *I understand that I am one moment away from a game-changing idea, a new connection, or a new opportunity.*
- *I understand that the past and the present are both fixed; they cannot be changed. The only thing that I can change is the future with the next steps I take.*
- *I understand to get anything I want in life, all I have to do is follow this process:*
    1. *Move into an aligned frame.*
    2. *Follow the process of life.*
    3. *Get the result.*
- *It's easy to follow the process of life because I get enjoyment following the process of life.*
- *I choose to believe this 100 percent, past, present, and future—all versions of me. And I take ownership of anything contradictory to this, and I integrate it completely now.*

Pause for three breaths.

Let's get into alignment with your full potential and capacity.

Repeat After Me (out loud):
- *I am ready to let go of all that holds me back.*
- *I am ready to explore my full potential, discover who I am, uncover and embrace my talents and gifts, and harness my superpowers.*
- *I embrace all of me. I embrace all the information that I haven't noticed in the past, and I own it fully as best I can today so I can share it with the world.*
- *It's safe for me to do that. It's why I'm on this planet right now.*

- *Even if the unknown feels a little scary, I'm going to automatically remember that it's just new and new is not bad. It's just new.*
- *I choose to explore my full potential as the infinite being I am.*
- *From this moment on, I choose to love and have gratitude for the path I took in my life to get here today.*
- *I choose to believe this 100 percent, past, present, and future—all versions of me. I take ownership of anything contradictory to this, and I integrate it completely now.*

Pause for three breaths.

Let's remove the most common fears people have...

Repeat After Me (out loud):

FEAR OF REJECTION

This Old Belief
- *If people don't like me, I feel rejected.*
- *If people don't accept me, I feel rejected.*
- *If people don't agree with me, what I'm presenting, or my ideas, I feel rejected.*
- *If someone tells me no, I feel rejected.*
- *And this belief will apply to anything else that has, does, or will make me feel rejected.*
- *This is my belief. I created it. I take full ownership of it.*
- *I integrate all of it now.*

This New Belief
- *If people don't like me, I do not feel rejected.*
- *If people don't accept me, I do not feel rejected.*

- *If people don't agree with me, what I'm presenting, or my ideas, I do not feel rejected.*
- *If someone tells me no, I do not feel rejected.*
- *Because if they don't want what I'm offering—that really has nothing to do with me. They just don't want it.*
- *Because the only time I can feel rejection is when I grow two more ears on my head.*
- *I choose to believe this 100 percent, past, present, and future—all versions of me. I take ownership of anything contradictory to this, and I integrate it completely now.*
- *I allow all of this to integrate smoothly.*

Pause for three breaths.

FEAR OF FAILURE

This Old Belief
- *If I miss my target, I feel failure.*
- *If I am wrong, I feel failure.*
- *If I don't get it right, I feel failure.*
- *If someone says no, I feel failure.*
- *And this belief applies to anything else that has, does, or will make me feel failure.*
- *This is my belief. I created it; I take full ownership of it, and I integrate all of it now.*

This New Belief
- *If I miss my target, I do not feel failure.*
- *If I am wrong, I do not feel failure.*
- *If I don't get it right, I do not feel failure.*
- *If someone says no, I do not feel failure.*
- *Because failure is how I learn.*
- *Because failure is how I grow.*
- *Because the only time I can feel failure is when I don't give it all I've got.*

- *I choose to believe this 100 percent, past, present, and future—all versions of me. I take ownership of anything contradictory to this, and I integrate it completely now.*
- *I allow all of this to integrate smoothly.*

Pause for three breaths.

FEAR OF NOT BEING LOVED

This Old Belief

- *I won't be loved.*
- *I won't be loved because I'm not good enough.*
- *I won't be loved because I have failed.*
- *I won't be loved if I'm single.*
- *I won't be loved if I don't have a partner.*
- *This is my belief. I created it, and I take full ownership of it.*
- *I integrate all of it now.*

This New Belief

- *I am loved.*
- *I am loved because I am good enough.*
- *I am loved because I have failed.*
- *I am loved if I'm single.*
- *I am loved if I don't have a partner.*
- *I am loved because I am alive.*
- *I am loved because I have friends.*
- *I am loved because I have people who love me.*
- *Because the only time I won't be loved is when I grow two more fingers on each hand and move to the planet Mercury for twenty-seven days.*
- *I choose to believe this 100 percent, past, present, and future—all versions of me. And I take ownership of anything contradictory to this and I integrate it completely now.*
- *I allow all of this to integrate smoothly.*

Pause for three breaths.

FEAR OF NOT BEING BEAUTIFUL

This Old Belief

- *I am not beautiful.*
- *I am not attractive.*
- *I am not thin enough to be beautiful and attractive.*
- *I am not in good enough shape to be beautiful and attractive.*
- *My body is not perfect or beautiful.*
- *I do not like my body.*
- *I do not love my body.*
- *This is my belief. I created it, and I take full ownership of it and I integrate all of it now.*

This New Belief

- *I am beautiful.*
- *I am attractive.*
- *I am beautiful and attractive regardless of how my body looks.*
- *I am in good enough shape to be beautiful and attractive.*
- *My body is perfect and beautiful.*
- *I like my body.*
- *I love my body.*
- *I am grateful for my body.*
- *Because the only time I am not beautiful or attractive is when I shrink to be six inches tall.*
- *I choose to believe this 100 percent, past, present, and future—all versions of me. I take ownership of anything contradictory to this, and I integrate it completely now.*
- *I allow all of this to integrate smoothly.*

Pause for three breaths.

FEAR OF WHAT OTHER PEOPLE THINK

This Old Belief

- *What other people think is more important than what I think.*
- *I need other people to like me.*
- *I can't like me unless other people like me.*
- *I feel dumb when people don't like what I say.*
- *I feel dumb when I am wrong.*
- *I feel dumb when people don't agree with what I say.*
- *This is my belief. I created it, and I take full ownership of it, and I integrate all of it now.*

This New Belief

- *What other people think is not more important than what I think.*
- *I do not need other people to like me.*
- *I like me regardless of other people's opinions.*
- *I do not feel dumb when people don't like what I say.*
- *I do not feel dumb when I am wrong.*
- *I do not feel dumb when people don't agree with what I say.*
- *I choose to believe this 100 percent, past, present, and future—all versions of me. I take ownership of anything contradictory to this, and I integrate it completely now.*
- *I allow all of this to integrate smoothly.*

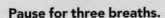

Pause for three breaths.

FEAR OF BEING TOO MUCH

This Old Belief

- *I am too much for other people.*
- *I can't do what I want because it's wrong.*
- *If I am myself, people will not like me.*
- *If I am myself, I will feel pain.*
- *If I am myself, I will be alone.*
- *If I am myself, I will not be successful.*
- *This is my belief. I created it, and I take full ownership of it, and I integrate all of it now.*

This New Belief
- *I am not too much for other people.*
- *I can't not do what I want because it's wrong.*
- *If I am myself, people will like me.*
- *If I am myself, I will not feel pain.*
- *If I am myself, I will not be alone.*
- *If I am myself, I will be successful.*
- *I choose to believe this 100 percent, past, present, and future—all versions of me. I take ownership of anything contradictory to this, and I integrate it completely now.*
- *I allow all of this to integrate smoothly.*

Pause for three breaths.

Let's get into alignment with what we want and deserve by redefining our relationship with success, self-worth, and happiness.

Repeat After Me (out loud):

SUCCESS

This Old Belief
- *I am not successful.*
- *I am not successful because I don't make enough money.*
- *I do not have enough to be successful.*
- *There are things I must do to become successful.*
- *I can't be successful yet.*
- *I can't be successful because of what I've done in the past.*
- *This is my belief. I created it, and I take full ownership of it, and I integrate all of it now.*

This New Belief

- *I am successful.*
- *I am successful regardless of how much money I make.*
- *I have enough to be successful.*
- *There are no things I must do to become successful.*
- *I can be successful.*
- *I can be successful because of what I've done in the past.*
- *I choose to believe this 100 percent, past, present, and future—all versions of me. I take ownership of anything contradictory to this, and I integrate it completely now.*
- *I allow all of this to integrate smoothly.*

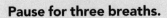

Pause for three breaths.

SELF-WORTH

This Old Belief

- *I am not worth it.*
- *I am not worth it because I have to take care of my responsibilities first.*
- *I am not worth it because I have work to do.*
- *Focusing on my happiness is being selfish.*
- *This is my belief. I created it, and I take full ownership of it, and I integrate all of it now.*

This New Belief

- *I am worth it.*
- *I am worth it because I have to take care of my responsibilities first.*
- *I am worth it because I have work to do.*
- *Focusing on my happiness is the best thing I can do.*
- *I choose to believe this 100 percent, past, present, and future—all versions of me. I take ownership of anything contradictory to this, and I integrate it completely now.*
- *I allow all of this to integrate smoothly*

Pause for three breaths.

HAPPINESS

This Old Belief

- *I am not happy.*
- *Happiness is not a part of success.*
- *Happiness is not a requirement for success.*
- *I do not have to be happy to be successful.*
- *I have to be successful before I can be happy.*
- *Focusing on happiness now is not a top priority.*
- *I can't be happy yet.*
- *I don't have time to focus on being happy.*
- *This is my belief. I created it, and I take full ownership of it, and I integrate all of it now.*

This New Belief

- *I am happy.*
- *Happiness is a part of success.*
- *Happiness is a requirement for real success.*
- *I can be happy to be successful.*
- *I don't have to be successful before I can be happy.*
- *Focusing on happiness now is a priority.*
- *I can be happy now; I love being happy now.*
- *I have time to focus on being happy.*
- *Happiness is a stabilizer and amplifier. It makes everything better.*
- *Happiness is important.*
- *Happiness increases my power.*
- *Happiness increases my impact.*
- *Happiness increases my alignment with life.*
- *Happiness increases my stability.*
- *Happiness anchors me in flow.*
- *Happiness is important to me.*
- *Happiness is a priority.*
- *I choose to believe this 100 percent, past, present, and future—all versions of me. And I take ownership of anything contradictory to this, and I integrate it completely now.*
- *I allow all of this to integrate smoothly.*

These New Beliefs

- *I am infinite.*
- *I believe in me.*
- *I live in certainty.*
- *I live in flow.*
- *I am in alignment with life.*
- *I love me.*
- *I love my past.*
- *I love my present.*
- *I love my future.*
- *I forgive everyone.*
- *I forgive myself.*

Pause for three breaths.

These New Beliefs

- *Everywhere I look, I see possibility.*
- *Everywhere I look, I see hope.*
- *Everywhere I look, I see happiness.*
- *Everywhere I look, I see love and joy.*
- *Everywhere I look, I see opportunities.*
- *Everywhere I look, I see kindness.*
- *Everywhere I look, I see money.*
- *Everywhere I look, I see clarity.*
- *Everywhere I look, I see positive change.*
- *Everywhere I look, I see people helping.*
- *Everywhere I look, I see love.*

Pause for three breaths.

- *I allow:*
  - *A life of joy.*
  - *A life of love.*
  - *A life of expansion.*
  - *A life of success.*
  - *A life of wonder.*
  - *A life of friendship.*
  - *A life of adventure.*
  - *A life of kindness.*
  - *A life of connection.*
  - *A life of magic.*
- *I allow the real me out.*
- *I allow myself to be the real me.*
- *I allow myself to follow my passion.*
- *I hear my passion.*
- *I see my passion.*
- *I see my path.*
- *I know my path.*
- *I hear my knowing.*
- *I hear my thinking.*
- *I easily know the difference between knowing and thinking.*
- *I know the way.*
- *I know why I'm here.*
- *I choose to believe this 100 percent, past, present, and future—all versions of me. I take ownership of anything contradictory to this, and I integrate it completely now.*
- *I allow all of this to integrate smoothly.*

Pause for three breaths.

Let's get into alignment with yourself.

- *I take full ownership of my life and everything in it.*
- *I take full ownership of my reality and everything in it.*

- *I take full ownership of my emotions and everything in them.*
- *I take full ownership of my past and everything in it.*
- *I take full ownership of my energy and everything in it.*
- *I take full ownership of my power and everything in it.*
- *I am ready to release all that holds me back.*
- *I am ready to explore my full potential.*

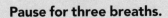

Pause for three breaths.

- *I am ready to become the real me, the whole me, nothing but me.*
- *I will not apologize for who I am.*
- *I will not play small to make other people feel better when they play small.*
- *I am on this planet right now for a purpose.*
- *This planet needs me for exactly who I am.*
- *I take full ownership of anything contradictory to this, and I integrate all of it now.*

Pause for three breaths.

- *I'm ready to discover and embrace who I really am.*
- *I'm ready to discover and embrace why I'm on this planet.*
- *I'm ready to discover and embrace my unique gifts and talents.*
- *I'm ready to discover and embrace my superpowers.*
- *I'm ready to discover and embrace all of me.*
- *I'm ready to follow my destiny, my unique path.*
- *I take on these new beliefs, even if they are scary because scary is just the feeling of expansion.*
- *Expanding is part of life.*
- *So, I no longer resist life.*

Pause for three breaths.

- *I do not resist my expansion in life.*
- *I look for expansion in my life.*
- *I look for what life is bringing me.*
- *From this moment on, I choose to work with life because life is always working for my highest and greatest good.*
- *Even if I can't see it at the time.*
- *Even if I have a period of challenge in my life.*
- *It means life is preparing me for something greater.*
- *I choose to believe that life is on my side, always working for my highest and greatest good.*

Pause for three breaths.

- *I choose to explore my full potential as a human being.*
- *I choose to move into internal alignment with myself..*
- *I choose to always become aware when I am out of alignment with myself.*
- *I choose to become in complete alignment with my past, my present, and my future.*

Pause for three breaths.

This Old Belief
- *I am not good enough.*
- *This is my belief. I created it. While this belief is attempting to help me, it's actually holding me back and hurting me. I am going to release it now. I'm not going to kill it or destroy it; I'm simply going to release it as I no longer need it.*
- *This is my belief. I created it. I take full ownership of it, and I integrate all of it now.*

Pause for three breaths.

This New Belief

- *I am good enough.*
- *I choose to believe it 100 percent.*
- *Because I was born this way.*
- *Because there's nothing wrong with me.*
- *I allow myself to be human.*
- *I choose to believe this 100 percent, past, present, and future—all versions of me. I take ownership of anything contradictory to this, and I integrate it completely now.*
- *I allow all of this to integrate smoothly.*

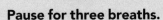

Pause for three breaths.

- *I take ownership of anything and everything that makes me judge myself, and I integrate all of it now.*
- *I take ownership of anything and everything that makes me judge myself about the past, and I integrate all of it now.*
- *I take ownership of anything and everything that makes me judge myself about the future, and I integrate all of it now.*
- *I take ownership of anything and everything that makes me judge myself about what I don't know, and I integrate all of it now.*
- *I take ownership of anything and everything that makes me judge myself about what I haven't done before, and I integrate all of it now.*
- *I take ownership of anything and everything that makes me feel limited, and I integrate all of it now.*
- *I take ownership of anything and everything that makes me doubt what is possible, and I integrate all of it now.*
- *I take ownership of anything and everything that makes me doubt what I'm capable of, and I integrate all of it now.*
- *I take ownership of anything and everything that makes me doubt that today will be permanent. I integrate all of it now.*
- *From this moment on, I choose to live in a reality where I always remember:*
  - *The past is not to be changed, only accepted for what it is.*
  - *In the past I did the best I could at the time, even though today I can see better options.*

- I choose to believe this 100 percent, past, present, and future—all versions of me. I take ownership of anything contradictory to this, and I integrate it completely now.
- I allow all of this to integrate smoothly.

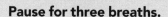

Pause for three breaths.

- I hereby forgive myself for everything in the past, that I did or did not do.
- I choose to love myself completely. Because I have things in my life today that I love dearly, and if my past had been any different, I wouldn't have those things I love in my life today.
- I choose to believe this 100 percent, past, present, and future—all versions of me. I take ownership of anything contradictory to this, and I integrate it completely now.
- I allow all of this to integrate smoothly.

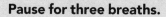

Pause for three breaths.

AND I SAY TO MYSELF

- I love you.
- I accept you.
- I am proud of you.
- You are enough; you always have been.
- You are wonderful and amazing.
- I love you.
- I love you.
- I choose to believe this 100 percent, past, present, and future—all versions of me. I take ownership of anything contradictory to this, and I integrate it completely now.
- I allow all of this to integrate smoothly.

Pause for three breaths.

Let's get into alignment with 10X growth.

Repeat After Me (out loud):

- *I take full ownership of all memories, beliefs, ideas, and experiences that:*
  - *Create negativity around accelerated growth.*
  - *Cause resistance to more work or more effort.*
  - *Cause resistance to a larger volume of work.*
  - *Cause resistance to a massive increase in volume of work.*
  - *Cause resistance to life flowing to me at an accelerated pace.*

Pause for three breaths.

- *I take full ownership of all memories, beliefs, ideas, and experiences of overwhelmingness, doubt, uncertainty, failure, fear, or any other negative emotions.*
- *And I release all of them now because I choose to understand the truth:*
  - *The overwhelmingness, doubt, uncertainty and failure were never problems.*
  - *They were just indicators that I had access to a higher frame.*
  - *In the past, I didn't know how to shift frames.*
- *I take full ownership of all the emotion, pain, struggle, and challenge I've had in my life that came from feeling overwhelmed and from doubt, uncertainty, failure, and fear. And I release all of that negative emotion now. And I allow myself to heal completely now because I'm a human being doing the best I can every moment of every day.*
- *I love my life right now, and I love the path I took to get here.*

- *I choose to believe this 100 percent, past, present, and future—all versions of me. I take ownership of anything contradictory to this, and I integrate it completely now.*
- *I allow all of this to integrate smoothly.*

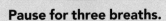

Pause for three breaths.

- *I take full ownership of any resistance I have to:*
  - *Doing more work.*
  - *Being overwhelmed.*
  - *Being in doubt.*
  - *Feeling uncertain.*
  - *Experiencing failure.*
  - *Taking on more than I can handle.*
  - *Taking on more than I know how to do.*
  - *Being out of control.*
- *And I integrate all of it now.*
- *Because I no longer resist the process of life. Because life is always unfolding for my highest and greatest good. The only way for me to experience the highs is to experience the lows. And if life gives me lows, it's because it's preparing me for something more amazing in the future.*
- *I love life. Experiencing life is the whole reason I'm here.*

Pause for three breaths.

- *I'm done being comfortable; I'm ready to be uncomfortable again.*
- *Bring it on.*
- *Because if I ever experience too much discomfort, I can just take another break. But now it is time to grow, so I hereby let life flow through me 100 percent. And I remove all filters I had, or adopted, or was conditioned to believe about how life should flow through me. Because the challenge that life brings me is for the purpose of turning me into who I'm supposed to become.*

- *The challenges life is presenting to me are for the purpose of bringing me to my destiny.*
- *I embrace myself.*
- *I embrace humanity.*
- *I allow life to flow through me 100 percent because if ever I feel overwhelmed, or have doubt, fear, uncertainty, or failure, all I have to say is I don't know what's next, probably something good.*
- *I choose to believe this 100 percent, past, present, and future—all versions of me. I take ownership of anything contradictory to this, and I integrate it completely now.*
- *I allow all of this to integrate smoothly.*

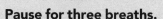

Pause for three breaths.

- *I take full ownership of my life and everything in it.*
- *From this moment on, what I choose to live in is a reality where accelerated growth is not an abnormal thing.*
- *Growth is growth. Small or big, it's just growth.*
- *Growth is just a target. Nothing is foreign to me.*
- *I can grow as fast or as slow as I want because I'm always in control.*
- *I see 10X growth all around me because I'm always surrounded by amazing people.*
- *Amazing people are always finding me.*
- *Amazing communities are always finding me.*
- *Life is always matching me up with amazing people.*
- *And the more I grow, the more I grow.*
- *I choose to believe this 100 percent, past, present, and future—all versions of me. I take ownership of anything contradictory to this, and I integrate it completely now.*
- *I allow all of this to integrate smoothly.*

Pause for three breaths.

Let's get into alignment with a higher financial mindset.

Repeat After Me (out loud):

- I choose to understand the truth about money—that money comes from other people. The only way I can get money is when someone gives it to me.
- I take full ownership of anything that is blocking me from receiving money fully, and I integrate all of it now.
- I take full ownership of any thoughts, memories, experiences, or social conditioning around money that limit me.
- I choose to understand that money is just energy, and in the next moment there's no limit to how much I can make. The amount of money I made yesterday is irrelevant because anything can happen next.
- I choose to understand that money can come from any direction at any time. There are an infinite number of ways that I could receive money.
- I choose to take full ownership of any limited perceptions about money that I lived with in the past, and I release it all now.
- I allow money to flow freely into my life.
- I allow money to flow freely into my life with ease now.
- I hereby remove all requirements to receiving money from my life.
- I allow money to flow into my life for any reason at any time in any volume.
- I understand that the amount of money I receive is a reflection of how much value I create. So from this moment on, I choose to live in a reality where my value to others is always increasing.
- I choose to live in a reality of infinite abundance, and even though I can't see it in this moment, I know money is on its way to me. Because that's the process of life.
- I choose to believe this 100 percent, past, present, and future—all versions of me. And I take ownership of anything contradictory to this, and I integrate it completely now.
- I allow all of this to integrate smoothly.

Pause for three breaths.

Let's move into complete integration.

Repeat After Me (out loud):

- *I take full ownership of anything else that needs processing or integration, and I integrate it completely now.*
- *I take full ownership of anything preventing me from allowing this session to be permanent, and I integrate it fully now.*
- *I take full ownership of all my thoughts and everything in them.*
- *I take full ownership of all my new understandings and everything else I've have been presented with.*
- *I take full ownership of everything I have forgotten, and I remember it all now.*
- *I take full ownership of everything I don't understand right now, and I understand all of it now.*
- *Every time I repeat this book or parts of it, its impact increases exponentially.*
- *I choose to believe this 100 percent, past, present, and future—all versions of me. I take ownership of anything contradictory to this, and I integrate it completely now.*
- *I allow all of this to integrate smoothly.*

Pause for three breaths.

Let's integrate with your true nature.

> **Repeat After Me (out loud):**
>
> - *I connect with the purest version of me there is.*
> - *I remove all my labels.*
> - *I remove all my beliefs.*
> - *I remove all my mental images.*
> - *I remove all I know about myself.*
> - *I feel who I am.*
> - *I feel who I really am.*
> - *I choose to feel who I really am.*
> - *I choose to know all that I am.*
> - *I choose to remember all that I am.*
> - *I choose to remember all that I was.*
> - *I choose to remember all that I've forgotten.*
> - *I choose to love all of me.*
> - *I choose to love everyone.*
> - *I choose to be free.*
> - *I choose to create my reality.*
> - *And so it is.*

WANT MORE? NEXT STEPS TO DO THE IMPOSSIBLE

If you want more of these concepts, I encourage you to visit my website, jason-dreescoaching.com. There you'll find numerous resources to help you take the next step and more information about the programs that are the pillars of Jason Drees Coaching. We offer one-on-one coaching, group coaching through several programs, most notably Mindset Academy and Mastermind groups, and we host live events throughout the year across North America.

The Jason Drees Coaching Instagram account is a great way to keep up with all the exciting things that are happening in the JDC world. My team would love to connect with you, so please reach out through the Jason Drees Coaching website or on social media.

Lastly, thank you for reading this book and pushing yourself to access the highest version of yourself.

From the bottom of my being, I truly believe this book will change your life if you put these concepts into practice. Keep it with you and read it again and again. I hope our unique paths cross beyond this book.

I promise you I will not stop exploring mindset and pushing the capabilities of human potential to shift frames and crush any target, no matter how impossible it may seem. I challenge you to do the same.

Epilogue

THE EVOLUTION OF MY PROCESS

I n case you didn't notice, this book is based on the evolution of my process and represents my current level of understanding. I continue to explore how to get what I want in life and the most impactful ways to teach others what I discover through coaching.

My work is genuinely fulfilling. Feeling authentically lucky every day, I find it is an honor to help people transform their lives. My journey of discovery continues to amaze me, and I'm extremely grateful for the opportunity to share it with you and my clients.

Because analyzing our operating system (our mindset) from inside the system is typically a foreign concept to most, one-on-one coaching can be an invaluable resource. When it comes to mindset shifting, an outside view of your current perspective is inherently more objective than your own evaluation. Just as our defining moments are only clear in retrospect, sometimes we are too close to our own behaviors and beliefs to produce an accurate inventory. That is where a coach can help.

Nothing inspires me more than working with clients and the Jason Drees Coaching community to develop a better understanding of their inner workings so that they can push their limits, remove resistance, and access their full potential. This is my unique path and my gift to the world. Whether you have found your passion, or it has yet to be uncovered, I hope this content will aid your own inspired journey, maximizing your effectiveness with ease and flow.

Discovering how life really works is a never-ending adventure, and there is always another level of awareness. Honestly, this used to frustrate me. Today, I love it.

As my understanding evolves and expands, so does my success. My enjoyment and satisfaction increase because I appreciate the journey by savoring the process of life and knowing that success is not the real target. Work is no longer a grind, because I followed my excitement, and it paid off. That's how I know the same is possible for you.

As new concepts are revealed, Jason Drees Coaching is evolving along with me.

I don't think the evolution of my process will ever end. I know my understanding of life is really just beginning. So, stay tuned for more. We are just getting started. My knowing indicates there is much more to come.

ACKNOWLEDGEMENTS

I would first like to acknowledge all the amazing clients I've had the privilege of working with. The work we did together created the foundation for this book.

I would also like to acknowledge Brandon Turner for always setting the bar high and continually being a role model of possibility. To Lucas Mitchell, the Wozniak I never knew I needed who allows me to stay in my lane of genius. I couldn't run JDC without you. Daniel Miller, for cold calling me when you did. MSA was the catalyst for the evolution of JDC and could never have happened without GenRevv. Ben Austin, I love that you showed up at exactly the right time, and I'm excited to see where life takes us—I know we have exciting adventures ahead. Stefanie Boicelli, I'm lucky to have you on the team; your legendary impact is growing by the moment.

Getting here was a lot easier because of the help, support, guidance, and coaching from: my mom and dad, Jennifer, Steve and Barbie, Marc Von Musser, Michael Savage, Dustin Runyon, Ian Clayton, Brodie Whitney, Roxanne Russell, Andrew Smith, Bonnie Hunter, Kamahl Barhoush, Matt Onofrio, Amy Ranae, Karen Chenaille, Jeff Harrison, Brittany Arnason, Kirk Jaffe, Rod Howard, Benjamin Beck, Joe Moffett, Benjamin White, John Creech, Dale Comontofski, Tim Smith, Dennis Crosby, Brent Alban, Jonathan Lang, Pasquale Zingarella, Kim Le, Larry Martin, Elaine and Nick Stageberg, Travis Lanning, Jen Khan, and all my other first 10Xers. Thank you to the BiggerPockets Publishing team—Savannah Wood, Kaylee Walterbach, and Katie Miller—as well as my editors, Janice Bryant and Elizabeth Frels, and my designer, Wendy Dunning.

More from
BiggerPockets Publishing

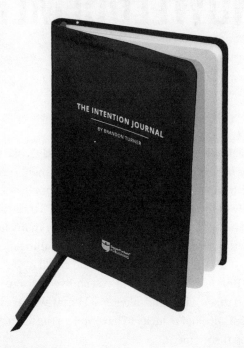

The Intention Journal

Some people can achieve great wealth, rock-solid relationships, age-defying health, and remarkable happiness—and so many others struggle, fail, and give up on their dreams, goals, and ambitions. Could it simply be that those who find success are more intentional about it? Once you build intentionality into your daily routine, you can achieve the incredible success that sometimes seems out of reach. Backed by the latest research in psychology, this daily planner offers an effective framework to set, review, and accomplish your goals.

If you enjoyed this book, we hope you'll take a moment to check out some of the other great material BiggerPockets offers. BiggerPockets is the real estate investing social network, marketplace, and information hub designed to help make you a smarter real estate investor through podcasts, books, blog posts, videos, forums, and more. Sign up today—it's free! **Visit www.BiggerPockets.com.**

Set for Life: Dominate Life, Money, and the American Dream

Looking for a plan to achieve financial freedom in just five to ten years? *Set for Life* is a detailed fiscal plan targeted at the median-income earner starting with few or no assets. It will walk you through three stages of finance, guiding you to your first $25,000 in tangible net worth, then to your first $100,000, and then to financial freedom. *Set for Life* will teach you how to build a lifestyle, career, and investment portfolio capable of supporting financial freedom to let you live the life of your dreams.

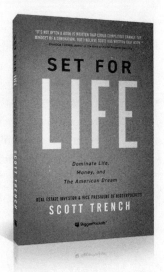

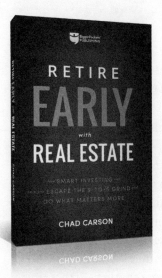

Retire Early with Real Estate

Escape the 9-to-5 work grind, retire early, and do more with your life! This book provides practical methods to quickly and safely build wealth using the time-tested vehicle of real estate rentals. Experienced real estate investor and early retiree, Chad Carson, shares the investment strategies that he used to create enough passive income to retire at 37 years old. Learn from more than twenty real estate investors and early retirees profiled in this book—retiring early is possible with a step-by-step strategy at hand!

More from
BiggerPockets Publishing

How to Invest in Real Estate

Two of the biggest names in the real estate world teamed up to write the most comprehensive manual ever written on getting started in the lucrative business of real estate investing. Joshua Dorkin and Brandon Turner give you an insider's look at the many different real estate niches and strategies so that you can find which one works best for you, your resources, and your goals.

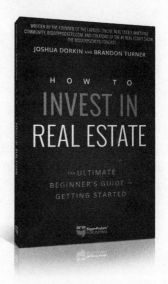

The Multifamily Millionaire, Volume I: Achieve Financial Freedom by Investing in Small Multifamily Real Estate

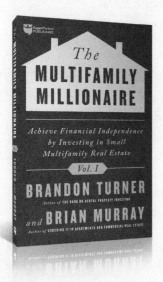

In this groundbreaking first volume of *The Multifamily Millionaire* series, experienced real estate investors Brandon Turner and Brian Murray share the step-by-step blueprint you need to get started with small multifamily real estate. No matter how much cash or experience you currently have, this book will take you on a journey through buying your first multifamily investment property and give you a framework for turning that single investment into long-term financial freedom.

The Book on Tax Strategies for the Savvy Real Estate Investor

Taxes! Boring and irritating, right? Perhaps. But if you want to succeed in real estate, your tax strategy will play a huge role in how fast you grow. A great tax strategy can save you thousands of dollars a year. A bad strategy could land you in legal trouble. With *The Book on Tax Strategies for the Savvy Real Estate Investor*, you'll find ways to deduct more, invest smarter, and pay far less to the IRS!

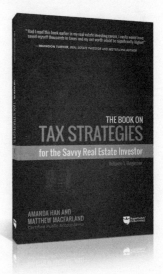

First-Time Home Buyer: The Complete Playbook to Avoiding Rookie Mistakes

Everything you need to buy your first home, from initial decisions all the way to the closing table! Scott Trench and Mindy Jensen of the *BiggerPockets Money Podcast* have been buying and selling houses for a collective thirty years. In this book, they'll give you a comprehensive overview of the home-buying process so you can consider all of your options and avoid pitfalls while jumping into the big, bad role of homeowner.

CONNECT WITH BIGGERPOCKETS

and Become Successful in Your Real Estate Business Today!

Facebook
/BiggerPockets

Instagram
@BiggerPockets

Twitter
@BiggerPockets

LinkedIn
/company/Bigger
Pockets

Website
BiggerPockets.com